Richard Le Gallienne led an abundant and wayward life. The grandson of a sea-captain and the son of a brewer, he was born in 1866 in Liverpool. After leaving home in 1887, he had a volume of poetry published privately. He moved to London in 1891 where he became a critic on the *Star* and was employed by John Lane as a reader for the Bodley Head. He was rapidly drawn into London literary life – in later years he was dubbed 'the golden boy of the nineties'. His poetry and critical works were widely read – notably *The Le Gallienne Book of English Verse,* published in 1922. Le Gallienne frequently travelled to Europe and from 1898, to America, where he settled in 1903. He moved to France permanently in 1931. He was married three times, had two daughters, and adopted a third. He died in Menton in the South of France in 1947.

Le Gallienne

*R*The ROMANTIC '90s

RICHARD LE GALLIENNE

WITH AN INTRODUCTION BY H. MONTGOMERY HYDE

ROBIN CLARK

Published in paperback by Robin Clark Limited 1993
A member of the Namara Group
27/29 Goodge Street, London W1P 1FD

A catalogue record for this book is available from the
British Library

ISBN 0 86072 158 2

Printed and bound in Great Britain by
BPCC Paperbacks Ltd
Member of BPCC Ltd

To
CHARLES HANSON TOWNE
'The onlie begetter' of the ensuing
harmless gossip of the last age,
true friend, true poet, with many
memories

INTRODUCTION

It has been the fashion to apply to the period of the eighteen-nineties in England such adjectives as "naughty," "decadent," "romantic," and "yellow." The term "romantic" was that chosen by the poet and essayist, Richard Le Gallienne, who was both in and of the period. In reality, however, all these epithets are merely different manifestations of this interesting epoch—what Sir Max Beerbohm has called "the Beardsley period," of which he is to-day the solitary survivor.

The literary and artistic group particularly associated with the 'nineties, which has been described by Le Gallienne and caricatured by "the incomparable Max," does not include by any means all the writers and artists who lived and flourished between the years 1890 and 1899, although Le Gallienne is more comprehensive in his writing of them in *The Romantic '90s* than Beerbohm is in his caricatures. It was indeed a group within a group. Tennyson, Swinburne and Meredith do not rightly belong to it, any more than Bernard Shaw, Wells, Kipling, Henry James and Thomas Hardy. The principal figure in this inner group, held by some to be its greatest character, was Aubrey Beardsley, the draughtsman of the *côterie*. Besides Beardsley, its artists were James McNeill Whistler, William Rothenstein, Charles Conder, Walter Sickert, Charles Ricketts, Charles Shannon and Max Beerbohm. Oscar Wilde was its dramatist and Arthur Symons its critic, while its poets, essayists and story-tellers included Ernest Dowson, Lionel Johnson, John Davidson, Stephen Phillips, Hubert Crackanthorpe, Ernest Rhys, Wilfred and Alice Meynell, Francis Thompson, Henry Harland, Mrs. George Egerton, William Sharp ("Fiona Macleod"), W. B. Yeats, George Moore, Lord Alfred Douglas and Richard Le Gallienne. John Lane, Elkin Mathews and Leonard Smithers were its publishers. Its characteristic periodicals were *The Yellow Book* and *The Savoy*. For most of its inspiration it looked to France and the so-called Symbolist movement in French literature.

Why have the 'nineties been regarded as "naughty"? In fact they were no more "naughty" than most other decades before and since, and considerably less so in expression than much, both in action and printed word, with which we are familiar to-day. The answer is that the 'nineties achieved a reputation for " naughtiness" through the art of shocking the middle classes of which the members of its peculiar group were assiduous exponents. Sex was discussed with a novel frankness in essays and fiction, while from the scientific standpoint the psychology of sex began to be exhaustively examined by Havelock Ellis, with unfortunate legal consequences as it turned out for himself. Many were attracted to the subject, among them Oscar Wilde particularly, by a craving for forbidden fruit, and the discussion of perverse practices not infrequently led to indulgence in them. Some members of the group became addicted to drugs, aping Verlaine, and others stimulated their senses by excessive consumption of alcohol. The favourite drink of the group was absinthe. Richard Le Gallienne relates how he made the acquaintance of this wondrous elixir on his first meeting with Lionel Johnson in the latter's rooms in Gray's Inn. Incidentally, it was Lionel Johnson who introduced Lord Alfred Douglas to Oscar Wilde, who was reported to drink absinthe nightly with his cronies in the Café Royal.

Épater le bourgeois—this was the current gospel, described as "one of the artless pastimes of artistic youth" by Le Gallienne, who added, that opportunities for shocking were greater then than now, when very little is left to do in that way. Wilde, in particular, as Le Gallienne reminds us, was always talking half-humorously of "purple sins," while his less distinguished imitators "loved to pose as mysteriously wicked." Yet, curiously enough, the cult of shocking the middle classes sprang from the middle classes themselves. "Nothing, not even conventional virtue, is so provincial as conventional vice," remarked Arthur Symons, "and the desire to 'bewilder the middle classes' is itself middle class." It was the achievement of the middle classes, not only that they should have produced much that was daring in the literary renaissance of the times, but that they should have been responsible during this same period for the spread of Socialism and the popularity of the safety bicycle. However, as Holbrook Jackson, a later critic of the period, has pointed out, the gospel of *épater le bourgeois* was in the main less an actuality than an idea seeking expression in life and using Art as its advocate.

The 'nineties have also been called "decadent." Indeed, many of the young writers and artists of the period openly rejoiced in this description. "It pleased some young men in various countries to call themselves Decadents," wrote Arthur Symons, "with all the thrill of unsatisfied virtue masquerading as uncomprehended vice." Properly speaking, the term should only be applied to style. But, as Symons has explained in a revealing essay on the subject, perversity of form and perversity of matter are no doubt often found together, and in some instances experiment was carried far into the field of sexual behaviour as well as into that of literary style.[1]

What, then, was the peculiar characteristic that made the writings of the 'nineties "decadent", or rather that particular portion of them with which this book is largely concerned? The qualities they exhibited have been summed up as perversity, artificiality, egoism and curiosity, while their novel ideas were reinforced by the use of epigram and paradox. It was a phase of artistic consciousness, an objective of self-expression thus depicted by Arthur Symons: "to fix the last fine shade, the quintessence of things, to fix it fleetingly; to be a disembodied voice, and yet the voice of a human soul; that is the ideal of Decadence." Perhaps no productions of the period carried these aims into execution with such striking effect as Wilde's perverse novel, *The Picture of Dorian Gray* and Beardsley's unfinished romance, *Under the Hill*, with its provocative illustrations. And it may be added, in passing, that discretion prompted Wilde to omit certain passages from the version of his work as it finally appeared in *Lippincott's Magazine*, while Beardsley's work is still generally available only in a drastically expurgated edition.

Richard Le Gallienne saw in "the will to romance"

[1] Arthur Symons: "The Decadent Movement in Literature," in *Harper's Monthly Magazine*, November, 1893.

the motive philosophy of the 'nineties. To his mind the representative writers and artists of the period sought to escape from the deadening thraldom of materialism and outworn conventions and "to live significantly—keenly and beautifully, personally and, if need be, daringly; to win from it its fullest satisfactions and most exhilarating experiences." This was romanticism indeed, but romanticism in the form of decadence. It was the culmination in England of the movement which had developed in France with the concept of personality in the Revolution a century before and which had reached the height of collective expression on the other side of the English Channel in the glorification of Napoleon. The English *fin-de-siècle* romantics certainly tended towards decadence. By continually satisfying new desires, they created new ones, and in the new thirst for fresh experiences and novel sensations they were insatiable to the point of exhaustion, mental and physical. Many of them, such as Beardsley, Wilde, Johnson and Dowson eventually turned to Rome and found ultimate satisfaction in the Catholic Church. Others, like the Irish poet W. B. Yeats, became theosophists. It is significant that the only convinced anti-mystic among them, John Davidson, committed suicide. The tired mood of the time, with its rejected hope, was perhaps best expressed by Ernest Dowson in his poem "Cynara", in which he saw the symbol of that joy and peace, unattained and possibly unattainable, which is the eternal dream of mankind:

> *I cried for madder music and for stronger wine,*
> *But when the feast is finished, and the lamps expire,*
> *Then falls thy shadow, Cynara! the night is thine;*

And I am desolate and sick of an old passion,
Yea hungry for the lips of my desire:
I have been faithful to thee, Cynara! in my fashion!

This decadent-romantic trend in English letters was to some extent shaken by the novelist Robert Hichens, whose book *The Green Carnation* satirized the manners and morals of its leaders with much the same effect as Gilbert and Sullivan had ridiculed the Aesthetic Movement in the previous decade in their comic opera *Patience*. The death blow was struck by the prosecution and conviction of Oscar Wilde at the Old Bailey in 1895, when "sins" which had till then been only darkly hinted at were now proved to have been actually committed. Public Opinion was more than shocked; it was outraged. The prevalent feeling was that this sort of thing had to stop, and, with Wilde's sensational trials, decadence in English art and letters came to an abrupt halt. In fact, decadence suddenly ceased to be fashionable, while the brilliant dramatist of the moment, who had been so savagely punished, realized the errors of his ways as he sat in an uncomfortable prison cell at Reading and composed that amazing saga of contrition and self-abasement, which his friend Robert Ross subsequently gave to the world under the title *De Profundis*.

The newspapers announced Wilde's downfall with the headlines ARREST OF OSCAR WILDE: YELLOW BOOK UNDER HIS ARM. Many people consequently jumped to the conclusion that the work in question was the famous quarterly *The Yellow Book*, which was edited by Henry Harland and Aubrey Beardsley and with which Richard Le Gallienne, as literary adviser to its publisher, John Lane, had been intimately associated. In the public mind *The Yellow Book* was regarded as the organ *par excellence* of the decadents, which to some extent it was, although, odd as it may appear, Oscar Wilde never contributed to its pages. Actually, the book which Wilde was carrying when he was taken by the detectives to Scotland Yard was not *The Yellow Book*, but *a* yellow book, *Aphrodite* by the French author Pierre Loüys, which happened to have a yellow cover. But the public, which was in no mood to make nice distinctions, proceeded to throw stones at the publisher's office windows. Though far from creditable to those who led it, the demonstration had its effect. "It killed *The Yellow Book*," Lane said afterwards, "and it nearly killed me."

But why should yellow have been the characteristic colour of the period? To some extent it was a reaction from the greens affected by the aesthetes, meeting the desire to have robust hues in the field of artistic production. Whistler employed it to effect both in his painting and in interior decoration. Thus there occurred what Le Gallienne in one of his *Prose Fancies* called "The Boom in Yellow." Bill-posters began to discuss the attractive qualities of the colour. "Who can ever forget meeting for the first time on a hoarding the Dudley Hardy's 'Yellow Girl'?" Then came *The Yellow Book*, which made its debut in April, 1894, with its light yellow jacket, from which one of Beardsley's typical female creations looked out in mocking laughter. "Nothing like *The Yellow Book* had been seen before," as Holbrook Jackson has written. "It was newness *in excelsis*: novelty naked and ashamed. People were puzzled and shocked and delighted, and yellow became the colour of the hour, the symbol of the time-spirit. It was associated with all that was *bizarre* and queer in art and life, with all that was outrageously modern." Yet it was never the intention of those who launched the new periodical that it should become what Arthur Waugh has aptly termed "the oriflamme of decadence." On the contrary, it was designed, in the words of its sponsors, to be "representative of the most cultured work which was being done in England, prose and poetry, criticism, fiction and art, the oldest school and the newest side by side, with no hall-mark except that of excellence and no prejudice against anything except dullness and incapacity." In addition to Henry Harland, Arthur Symons, John Davidson, George Moore and Richard Le Gallienne, its literary contributors included Henry James, A. C. Benson, William Watson, Richard Garnett and Edmund Gosse; and besides Aubrey Beardsley, William Rothenstein, Walter Sickert and Joseph Pennell, it boasted as illustrators Sir Frederick Leighton, J. T. Nettleship, Wilson Steer and Walter Crane.

The Yellow Book was superseded by the Yellow Press. With the check to the art movement of the 'nineties caused by the Wilde trials, Alfred Harmsworth seized the opportunity with the foundation of *The Daily Mail* to provide culture of a more popular kind for the masses. The gospel of Imperialism, degenerating into jingoism, was ardently preached by his organ, while Rudyard Kipling became the poet of the patriots. With this new development, or rather with its degeneracy, Richard Le Gallienne had little sympathy, any more than he sympathized with the degeneracy of the earlier school. One of the last things he wrote before departing for America was a critical study of Kipling, in which he blamed that poet, not altogether without justice, for the trend of thought which led to Mafeking Night. But this is to anticipate somewhat.

It was from beneath the sign of The Bodley Head in Vigo Street, off Regent Street, that the peculiarly characteristic works of the period issued in a steady stream. The firm owed its origin to the enterprise of a remarkable individual, John Lane, when he was working as a clerk in the Railway Clearing House at Euston. His ambition was to become the publisher of fine books. Along with a bookseller named Elkin Mathews, like himself a native of Devonshire, Lane opened a book shop in Vigo Street, over which he hung a sign showing the head of that greatest of bibliophiles, Sir Thomas Bodley, a sign which for many years was to be the hall-mark of the best craftsmanship in book production.

The first work to be published by Mathews and Lane was a book of poems by Richard Le Gallienne, called *Volumes In Folio*, which made its appearance towards the end of 1889. It was a thin little book in blue-grey boards with a white-panelled back and printed on hand-made paper. The publisher's faith in his first author was as great as his belief in the success of his business venture. To Lane at this time Le Gallienne appeared as "a young man of undoubted genius who was bound to set the Thames on fire, and whose face was that of a Greek God."

Le Gallienne, who was only twenty-three, had recently arrived in London from Liverpool and was employed in writing book reviews for *The Star*. Lane promptly made him the firm's reader. If he did not create quite the sensation which the publisher predicted, Le Gallienne certainly scored a remarkable success during the next dozen years. In addition to an interesting critical study of George Meredith, he poured out a stream of verse and literary criticisms which were widely read, and he also wrote a romantic novel *The Quest of the Golden Girl* which went into eighteen editions. This work was the most popular and characteristic book that its author wrote. In the words of Osbert Burdett, "all the influences that went to his making are to be found in it, and it confirms our opinion of him as the point of contact between the more recondite and the more popular literary aspirations of his time as the declining phase of the Romantic Movement. The book has been called, aptly enough, a new sentimental journey.... The adventures seem to threaten the conventions that they end by respecting, and the reader feels like one of the seven heroines, in doubt whether to be grateful or disappointed at the happy issue of her fears. It might have shocked Queen Victoria. It might have seemed tame to Marie Bashkirtsheff. To the wider public of the 'nineties, which was mostly far from either of these extremes, it was tantalizingly perfect. The incident, familiar in Gautier, of the girl who wears the clothes of a youth in order to accompany a charming stranger on a walking tour, exactly hit the taste of the age when the New Woman on the horizon had become the girl with a bicycle in the street. ... To have the sensation without the danger is exactly what conventional people desire."

Le Gallienne thus became a spear-head of the

literary movement which Lane and Mathews, not-withstanding the eventual dissolution of their partner-ship towards the end of 1894, did so much to translate into action. As the firm's reader and literary adviser, he was able to recommend the manuscripts of many young writers for publication. Actually the Bodley Head added some already established authors to its list, like Oscar Wilde and Henry James, but there were others whose literary careers owed much to Le Gallienne's intervention, poets like Francis Thompson and W. B. Yeats, and prose writers such as Lionel Johnson, Mrs. George Egerton and George Moore.

John Lane, while genuinely fond of poetry, was convinced that it could be made to pay, a view which most of his brother publishers did not share at that time. Le Gallienne helped him to succeed in making it pay. The authors to their own intense irritation, were popularly alluded to at the time as "minor poets," to distinguish them in the middle class imagination from such poetic giants as Tennyson and Browning.

As for Le Gallienne himself, he had all the physical attributes which a poet is popularly supposed to possess. He looked, in William Rothenstein's words, "like Botticelli's Head of Lorenzo." His handsome features, long hair and unconventional clothes—he usually wore a green velveteen jacket and a flowing black tie—gave him the appearance of a poet, or at least what his young female readers thought a poet should look like. These readers would cherish his picture between the leaves of one of his slim volumes of verse. To do him justice, if his poetic writing cannot be classed as great, there was nothing decadent about it, any more than decadence characterized his moral behaviour. He was indeed consummately masculine; he had the biceps of a blacksmith and could use his fists. If he was in sympathy with some of the literary achievements of the decadent school he endeavoured to avoid its excesses. The weakness of his work is that it reflects too much a combination of sentiment and sensuousness. However, as Osbert Burdett writes, "his double sympathies made him an invaluable interpreter of the writers of his time, and this service can hardly be emphasized too strongly since the evidence for it is necessarily the cherished recollection of those who do not tell all they know to the general public." He had no leanings towards what he called, in one of his poems, "strange-coloured vice." His emphasis was on purer forms of romance. Richard Le Gallienne was to the 'nineties what Rupert Brooke was to the succeeding generation of poetry readers. The only difference was that he did not die young, but emigrated to America at the height of his success and lived on to a charming and dignified old age in France.

In his account of the period and its typical personalities, which he wrote when approaching sixty and called *The Romantic '90s*, Le Gallienne has little to say about himself. He was content to leave autobiography, as he put it, to "men who are still in love with their egos, that wondrous love affair which is apt to outlive all others." It is well, therefore, to set out the main facts of his life.

Richard Le Gallienne was born in Liverpool on January 20, 1866, the eldest son of John and Jane Gallienne. His ancestors had lived in the Channel

Islands for more than three centuries, and his paternal grandfather, the first of the family to settle in England, was a Guernsey sea captain. Thus, when he added the prefix "Le" to his surname on the title page of his first published poems, he was merely reverting to the style of his Guernsey forbears.

His father, John Gallienne, was the manager and secretary of the Birkenhead Brewery Company. From him he inherited an interest in theology; from his mother, a passion for poetry. He went to school at Liverpool College and oddly enough it was as a prize for divinity there that he received his first volume of verse, the works of the poet laureate, Lord Tennyson. As a youth he haunted the Liverpool booksellers, particularly Walmsley's shop in Lord Street, because it had published the "Epigrams" of another budding poet of the city, William Watson, whom he admired.

His father wanted him to be an accountant and apprenticed him to a Liverpool firm of chartered accountants, Chalmers, Wade and Company. He served the seven years of his articles in their offices in Fenwick Street, but he found the drudgery of accountancy most distasteful, and failed to pass the necessary examinations. His interests were entirely literary. He wanted to become a poet, and his mother encouraged his latent poetic talents. With her assistance he took a loft in an old office building near the docks and here began to scribble boyish verses. A poem which he sent to the American writer, Oliver Wendell Holmes, brought back an encouraging four-page letter—reproduced in the following pages—in which the eminent Bostonian wished his youthful correspondent "all success in your career as a book-fancier and a man of letters." Dr.

Holmes was also gracious enough to look him up when passing through Liverpool some months]ater.

Some of his friends in the accountant's office clubbed together to get his first collection of poems published in a privately printed edition. They appeared in 1887 under the title, *My Ladies' Sonnets, and other Poems*. Meanwhile young Richard lectured to Merseyside literary societies, stimulated by the appearance at this time of Oscar Wilde whom he heard addressing an audience at Birkenhead on his "Impressions of America." To this lecture, in which Wilde described some of his own experiences on a lecture tour there, may be traced Le Gallienne's interest in the United States, which led him to visit the country some years later and eventually to settle there. At the same time Le Gallienne was frequently seen in the pulpits of local churches and chapels in the rôle of a lay preacher. In one Unitarian Church it is said that he caused considerable raising of eyebrows by remarking: "Some there are who admire the music of the spheres. Some there are who admire Lottie Collins. Happy are they who can admire both!" (Lottie Collins was a popular music hall artiste who scored a great hit by her singing of "Ta-ra-ra-boom-de-ay" with its catchy chorus.) One of Le Gallienne's sermons was subsequently published —"If I Were God, by Richard Le Gallienne." This provoked an irreverent reviewer of this effort to remark, "If I were Richard Le Gallienne, by God I'd get my hair cut."

In the same year as Le Gallienne's first book of poems made its appearance, Wilson Barrett, the well-known actor-manager and author of the highly successful drama, *The Sign of the Cross*, was playing in

Liverpool. The story goes that the young poet waited outside the stage door one night, and when the actor had come out and got into a hansom cab, Le Gallienne pursued the hansom on foot, succeeded in stopping it, and introduced himself with such a persuasive charm that Wilson Barrett offered to take him south and employ him in London. Le Gallienne did not accept the offer immediately. When, however, he heard that he had failed in the final examination to qualify as a chartered accountant, Richard went to London to work in the post which he had been offered. With him went the comedian, James Welch, who was later to marry his sister. They had only £9 between them, and though Welch was eventually down to his last sixpence, Wilson Barrett also found him a job, giving him a part in one of his productions at the Globe Theatre. As for young Richard, his association with the actor-manager lasted only for a few months, but it was long enough to introduce him to the world he wished to know—the world of Swinburne and George Meredith, the London Theatre and Fleet Street. But he did not accompany Wilson Barrett to America, apparently because he thought the change of climate would aggravate the asthma from which he suffered. When he eventually crossed the Atlantic for the first time some years later, he discovered that the complaint which had troubled him in England did not affect him in New York.

After Wilson Barrett's departure, Le Gallienne got work reviewing books for *The Star*, the London evening newspaper, then edited by T. P. O'Connor. His column was called "Books and Bookman" and his contributions appeared over the signature "Log-roller". Along with Ernest Dowson, Lionel Johnson, Arthur Symons, W. B. Yeats and others, he became one of the original members of the Rhymer's Club, which used to meet at Dr. Johnson's favourite tavern "The Cheshire Cheese," in Le Gallienne's words, "for discreet conviviality, conversation on literary matters, and the reading of their own new book lyrics," or, as Arthur Symons put it, "where long clay pipes lay in slim heaps on the tables between tankards of ale, and young poets, then very young, recited their verses to one another with a desperate and ineffectual attempt to get into tune with the Latin Quarter." His second book of poems had already been accepted by John Lane, and he was soon installed beneath the sign of the Bodley Head reading manuscripts for the new firm of publishers. Many of these, which Le Gallienne picked out and recommended for publication, were to become valuable both for the authors and the publisher.

Before leaving Liverpool Le Gallienne had met the woman who was to become his first wife. Every day he and his friends in the accountant's office used to take their luncheon in Miss Macpherson's café in Tithebarn Street. The waitress, who used to serve them, was a pretty girl called Mildred Lee. One day she said she could not attend to their table any more. The reason was that she had fallen in love with young Le Gallienne. Fortunately for her, he returned her feeling, and in 1891 they got married. They were supremely happy together at Mulberry Cottage, their home in Brentford, but their happiness lasted for only three years. Mildred died in giving birth to their daughter, Hesper Joyce[1]. It was a blow which completely un-

[1] Mrs. Robert Hare Hutchinson.

settled the husband and from which in a sense he never recovered. Frederic Chapman, a colleague at the Bodley Head, came down to the house next day and walked the neighbouring lanes all that night with Le Gallienne to tire him out, because he could not sleep.

His fine poem "Song," which originally appeared in *The Yellow Book*, was inspired by her memory:

> *She's somewhere in the sunlight strong*
> *Her tears are in the falling rain,*
> *She calls me in the wind's soft song.*
> *And with the flowers she comes again;*
>
> *Yon bird is but her messenger,*
> *The moon is but her silver car,*
> *Yea! sun and moon are sent by her*
> *And every wistful, waiting star.*

The wound was still fresh when, some years later, he wrote the sonnet which he called "Home":

> *"We're going home!" I heard two lovers say,*
> *They kissed their friends and bade them bright goodbyes;*
> *I hid the deadly hunger in my eyes*
> *And, lest I might have killed them, turned away.*
> *Ah, love, we too once gambolled home as they,*
> *Home from the town with such fair merchandise—*
> *Wine and great grapes—the happy lover buys:*
> *A little cosy feast to crown the day.*
> *Yes! we had once a heaven we called a home,*
> *Its empty rooms still haunt me like thine eyes*
> *When the last sunset softly faded there;*
> *Each day I tread each empty haunted room,*
> *And now and then a little baby cries,*
> *Or laughs a lovely laughter worse to bear.*

Henceforth he was consumed by a certain inborn restlessness which determined him eventually to seek fresh fields. In 1895 he accompanied John Lane on a business trip to New York, and he was there when the Wilde scandal took place. This was a source of lasting sorrow to him and acute embarrassment to Lane, since the name of a young man employed in the Bodley Head offices, Edward Shelley, figured prominently in the trials as a witness for the prosecution. Lane, who was quite unjustly accused of having introduced this young man to Wilde, thereupon anticipated the cable demand of William Watson and Wilfred Meynell by withdrawing all Wilde's books which the firm had published. At the same time the offices in Vigo Street were the object of attack caused by ill-will toward *The Yellow Book*, as already described, and Aubrey Beardsley, as art editor, shared in the opprobrium. "Nothing has happened here to justify the action," wrote Lane to Frederic Chapman, "and it seems to me a great injustice to Beardsley. So think Kipling, Le Gallienne and Tree."

Two years later Le Gallienne married his second wife, Julie Norregaard. Their only child was a daughter, Eva, who was destined to become well-known as an actress and dramatic producer in the United States. But this marriage was not a success, and later Le Gallienne and his second wife separated, Julie Le Gallienne going to Paris and taking Eva with her, and Richard making the final break with England and settling in New York. He did not see his daughter again until 1915, when she made her first appearance on the American stage as a negro servant in a play called *Mrs. Boltay's Daughters*. Legend has it that Le

Gallienne saw Eva's name on the playbill and promptly bought a ticket for the show. When she appeared with a blackened face, he was heard exclaiming aloud in the theatre, "My God! Is that my daughter?"

Le Gallienne, who had also visited America in 1898, as well as in 1895, surprised his friends this time by staying there. In characteristic verse Sir Max Beerbohm begged him to return, but his happy call met with no response.

> *Oh, witched by American bars,*
> *Pan whistles you home on his pipes,*
> *We love you for loving the stars,*
> *But what can you see in the stripes?*

Richard Le Gallienne never returned to England, except for one short visit when he spent a week with his relations near Liverpool. He made many friends in the United States, where he wrote fitfully for American newspapers and magazines. These poems and essays would be collected from time to time and make their appearance in book form from the Bodley Head, but London knew him no more.

When his *New Poems* were published in 1910, Mr. Arthur Waugh reviewed the collection with a strong touch of nostalgia. "A new volume of poems by Mr. Le Gallienne bearing the imprint of the Bodley Head, comes like a faint but haunting echo of the past when we were all younger," he wrote. "Is it really fifteen years since the Rhymers' Club was broken up? And who remembers their melodies now? Mr. Yeats has fled to Ireland—a country from which he only issued, as it were, a changeling—but what should Mr. Le

Gallienne do in America? Fifteen years ago he could scarcely have imagined a less congenial soil. How should he sing the Lord's song in a strange land? Mr. Ernest Rhys is busy editing learned classics for the million, and only too seldom stringing his Celtic lyre to music. Mr. Arthur Symons is unhappily ill. The deaths of Lionel Johnson and Ernest Dowson are bitterly fresh in the memory. All the little company is scattered, and Mr. Le Gallienne's re-appearance from under the old Bodley Head bust seems like some strange survival of forgotten associations. No reviewer of sensibility who remembers the age of the Rhymers and the youth of *The Yellow Book* will open this inviting volume without a touch of sentiment.

"Of course, they had their weaknesses and affectations, these Rhymers of our youth. They were none of them above riding their Pegasus through the public streets, and some even assumed a Viking air of conquest in flowing locks and wild gesticulations. But, after all, they did care. They did care very much for poetry, and there was something infectious about their enthusiasm, for they made other people care as well. . . . And now out of the general silence Mr. Le Gallienne has returned, and the delightful thing about his return is the growing certainty, which increases as we wander through his pages, that however much we have changed, he is still essentially the same. But not even America—metallic, commercial, hustling America— has been able to work withering miracles upon his idealism. He is the same poet of wayward sentiment and unpopular loyalty, true as ever to the golden gods and pearly dawns, the apple blossom and wind-blown love-locks as in the summers of fifteen or seventeen years ago; not a whit (thank the Muses!) more sophisticated."

Here is a typical poem of this middle period:

All the loving ever done
Is not so sweet as the kiss o' the sun
Nor a woman ever born,
As good to look on as the morn.
Up, my soul, and let's away
Over the hills at break of day,
Following, whate'er befalls,
Yonder fairy horn that calls,
Angel-blown in yonder star.
Better far, O better far,
Better far than any girl,
Is the morning's face of pearl
And the wind about our ears—
The true music of the spheres
And the running of the river
Good to listen to for ever.

For a long time Le Gallienne lived in New York; from there he removed to Darien, Connecticut, and thence to Woodstock, New York. After his separation from Julie Norregaard, he married Irma Stuart-Hinton, who acted under the stage name of Irma Perry. A daughter Gwen has achieved a reputation as a painter, particularly of portraits.

After the First World War, Le Gallienne and his wife went to live for a time in Paris, and here he found inspiration to write his book on the 'nineties, which was originally published in 1926. He dearly loved France and its beautiful capital. "No place on earth has been so fearfully and wonderfully lived in," he wrote.

"No city has been more saturated with human experience." He also wrote much about France during this period. In 1929, he began to contribute a weekly column to *The New York Sun* entitled "From a Paris Garret." These articles were republished as a book some years later, and with it the author gained a special award from the French Government for the best book of the year about France written by a foreigner.

Some time previously Le Gallienne had severed his remaining connections with America and had decided to settle, as he put it "from now on till the end of the story" in a romantic two-centuries-old villa which he had acquired between the old town of Mentone and the Italian border, at the foot of the Maritime Alps, with the Mediterranean brimming in at his windows. But he was not fated to live in that lovely place till "the end of the story." The occupation of Mentone by the Italians in the summer of 1940 drove him and his wife to seek sanctuary in the nearby principality of Monaco. Here they lived, it would be truer to say survived, until the liberation—he once fainted in the street in Monte Carlo from lack of food.

He was repeatedly approached both by the German and by the Italian authorities in the area, who were anxious to enlist his services for propaganda against the Allies, but he rejected with scorn all offers of this kind. Had he yielded, of course, he might have lived in comfort, if not in affluence, and his life might conceivably have been prolonged. That his courageous attitude was respected by the enemy appears from the fact that a high-ranking German officer refused to allow a subordinate, who was in occupation of his villa, to transport the poet's library as spoils of war to Germany.

Back again in Mentone after the liberation, Le Gallienne found that the villa was too badly damaged to live in again, but he found another in the neighbourhood, the Villa Beatrice, into which he moved the remains of his library. Here, in his book-lined study, with a fine view from the windows of the Alps and the sea across palm trees and orange groves, I talked with him in the summer of 1947, a few weeks before his death. There was a certain happiness and serenity of manner about him, which struck me very forcibly at the time. Though old in years—he was eighty-one— he seemed young—"incorrigibly young," as he put it. "I simply cannot be sensible and grow up," he said. "I don't know how it's done and never mean to try." He spoke much in a soft silvery voice of the 'nineties and the literary figures of the period.

In the course of our conversation he saw my eye fall on a small wooden table in one corner of the room. He hastened to explain that he had bought it at a sale of the effects of the Hotel d'Alsace, the small hotel on the left bank of the river Seine in Paris, where Oscar Wilde had died. It had been in his bedroom there, and Wilde had used it as a writing table during the last months of his life.

Richard Le Gallienne died suddenly but quite peacefully in his sleep on September 15, 1947. At the simple funeral service which followed, his friend Grant Richards, the publisher, read his poem "What of the Darkness?" with its characteristically expressive lines:

> *And is it true indeed, and must you go,*
> *Set out alone across the moorland track.*
> *No love avail, though we have loved you so,*

No voice have any power to call you back?
And losing hands stretch after you in vain,
And all our eyes grow empty for your lack,
Nor hands, nor eyes, know aught of you again.

The poet's last resting place is in the cemetery high up amongst the eucalyptus trees and orange groves, above Mentone, and near the grave of that other striking figure of the 'nineties, Aubrey Beardsley, perhaps Le Gallienne's greatest artistic contemporary, who died in the same town almost half a century before.

Shortly afterwards I was privileged to broadcast an obituary appreciation of the poet in the Third Programme of the B.B.C. It ended with the following words, with which I feel I cannot do better than commend *The Romantic* '90s to a new and, I hope, even wider circle of readers than the book enjoyed on its first publication.

"Richard Le Gallienne lived a rich and profitable life, whose value may be assessed not so much in terms of bank balances and royalties, but in his creative work, in his constructive literary criticism, in the help and encouragement of which he gave so generously to other writers, and, above all, in his romantic spirit and his ever abundant kindness and understanding. For these qualities he will always live in the hearts of his friends, and wherever what is fine in letters is appreciated."

H. MONTGOMERY HYDE.

THE ROMANTIC '90s

Charley of trans-Atlantic fame,
  Who, oft o'er trans-Atlantic brew,
Prompted these tales—yours the bright blame
  I print them, dedicate to you:
  Days still so near and still so new,
Those days of Beardsley and of Wilde,
  So innocent and filled with dew!—
When this old world was still a child.

Those yellow naughty days so tame,
  When all we do now was still to do,
And "sin" still wore the skirts of shame,
  And bare-legged ladies, far and few,
  Our unaccustomed glances drew;
And our transgressions were so mild,
  I blush to think of them—don't you?—
When this old world was still a child.

Innocent '90s! when some name
  Immortal I a moment knew,
Touched the great robe already flame,
  Watched the last eagle in the blue
  Augustly vanish, bade adieu
To the great Past, worshipped and smiled
  With Youth that had its greatness too—
When this old world was still a child.

ENVOI.

Charles, though the Past from which it grew
  By the pert Present be denied—
Youth loves "the '90s," *entre nous!*—
  When this old world was still a child.

RICHARD LE GALLIENNE

I

Ah! did you once see Shelley plain,
And did he stop and speak to you,
And did you speak to him again?
How strange it seems and new!

THE reader must not fear that I am going to write my autobiography. No, I leave that to men still in love with their own egos, that wondrous love affair which is apt to outlive all others. Something of myself, indeed, I shall be obliged here and there to bring in to make a background for these random memories of a period, in which, in spite of the alleged irreverence of the present generation, I have found, in talking to younger people, a surprisingly enthusiastic interest; but that something shall be as little as possible. As I once wrote in a book for William Watson:

These to thee, Will, from critic to creator—
My only greatness is to praise the greater.

A sentiment, I hope, of commendable modesty. And, by the way, I should have said *Sir* William Watson, for most of my early friends seem to have become knights. Who was it, by the way, who said that "London is now a City of Dreadful Knights"?

When I was a boy poets were comparatively rare beings, and Poetry Societies were all but unknown blessings. There was a Browning Society, and later a Rhymers' Club, of which I shall have to speak; but those were about all. Poets were still mysterious beings, and to meet one was a thrilling experience. No one glibly called himself or herself a poet. There was still an old-world sentiment, as Mrs. Browning wrote, that

> *that name is royal*
> *And to wear it like a queen I dare not.*

Such indeed was my state of innocence, in my schooldays in Liverpool, that when a friendly schoolmaster took me into a bookshop to buy a Virgil, and pointing to a volume on the counter, said: "This is Mr. Swinburne's new volume," I provoked his laughter by asking: "Are there poets still alive?"—for, to tell a truth which may well seem incredible to-day, I had a notion that poets were mythical beings, who lived in an earlier age of the world, an illusion which, I need hardly say, I was not long to preserve. That, as I say, was in Liverpool, a city which might well excuse the mistake.

Yet, apart from those happy personal memories which the most prosaic city must have for one born there, Liverpool, before I left it, had given me my first thrilling glimpse of embodied fame. In its Adelphi Hotel I once had tea with Dr. Oliver Wendell Holmes. It was in 1886, and England, which adored his writings, was fêting him with something like royal honours. In those days I was an enthusiastic bibliophile, and among my treasures was an Elzevir edition of the Colloquies of Erasmus, which, to my delight, one day, in reading "The Professor at the Breakfast Table," I discovered was identical with the Elzevir mentioned in that book. The discovery resulted in a piece of boyish doggerel about Elzevirs which was printed in a bookish magazine, and which I sent, with a letter, to Doctor Holmes. Only a bookish lad of nineteen can experience the joy with which some weeks afterwards I received a letter of four pages from my Boston hero written in his own hand. I reproduce it here for the benefit of bibliophiles, and those who are sensible enough still to read one of the most vivacious and stimulating of *causeurs*. Doctor Holmes was then seventy-seven, and the fact that he should take the trouble to write four pages to an unknown boy across the sea speaks no little for the kindness of his heart.

BOSTON, *March* 5, 1886.

MY DEAR SIR,

I confess that your letter frightened me. I am gradually coming to the conclusion that I cannot keep up my correspondence without sacrificing so much of my time and strength as to incapacitate me from any effective literary labour. A large part of every day has to be sacrificed in replying to correspondence and in acknowledging the books and pamphlets of all sorts and sizes which every day brings me. However, I did read your letter, and, of course, I found it interesting. First, I was pleased to know that you liked my writings. We are all human, more or less, and most of us like to be acceptable to our fellow-mortals. Then it is a comfort to be told that one's writings have solaced, instructed, entertained, or even amused one's unknown friends. I get a great many letters that tell me such things and I cannot say that I have ever got tired of them. So on this ground I thank you. I enjoyed your verses, too, and I lived over with you the delight of your first sight of an *imprimatur*. The little compliment to myself did not make them less palatable. I not only like your poem, but I am pleased to recognize a brother bibliophile. I have a few rare books in my library of five or six thousand—some *incunabula*—the best, *not* my oldest, a Nicholas Jenson of 1481—a Valerius Maximus of 1474, etc., etc., a few Aldi—a number of Elzevirs, etc., but I only care for a few specimens and am not a collector. I picked up in Lyons, fifty years ago, a copy of the Aphorisms of Hippocrates edited by *Rabelais*, with his original Preface, from which I extracted a motto for the Rabelais Club of London. Well, I wish you all success in your career as a book-fancier and a man of letters. I thank you, particularly for the two charming little volumes of Wordsworth's Poems, which I much fancy.

But you must not depend on me as a correspondent, for I am entirely unequal to the labour my unknown friends lay upon me. I thank them none the less for their kind expressions.

> Believe me, my dear sir,
> Sincerely yours,
>   OLIVER WENDELL HOLMES.

It was some three months after this that Doctor Holmes visited England, and he wrote me a note from London inviting me to call on him at Liverpool on his way back to America. Never shall I forget his quaint tiny figure, with his humour-saturated face, seamed all over like a withered apple, and the exquisite courtliness of his welcome to me, as I sat with him, scarce able to believe it was really he, "over the tea-cups," that legendary afternoon.

Soon after that I was to perpetrate a very youthful volume of verse which introduced me to Mr. John Lane, and so took me to London, where Mr. Ernest Parke, then editor of the *Star*—the first editor my awe-struck eyes had beheld and the most genial—gave me my earliest job, the writing of a "Books and Bookmen" column, which up to that time had been written by Mr. Clement Shorter, who had just ascended to higher spheres as the editor of the *Illustrated London News*—spheres in which he is still happily active, as he well may be, not yet having attained to any considerable antiquity. I am proud to think that among my colleagues were the distinguished dramatic critic, Mr. A. B. Walkley, and Mr. Bernard Shaw, who wrote musical criticism, over the initials "C. di B." (Corno di Bassetto)—neither gentleman having yet, even now, attained to the age of knighthood. On my coming to London I brought with me the manuscript of a book on George Meredith, which was soon published by Mr. Lane, who also invited me to be his "reader"— many since famous manuscripts thus passing through my hands. I was thus fairly launched into that literary world, which in Liverpool had seemed a far-off dream. A young man who is at once a reviewer for a great newspaper and a publisher's reader will not long remain without friends, though he may occasionally, in cynical moments, wonder how much he is loved for himself—and how much for his reviews!

Which reminds me of a saying of Mr. George Moore's on the only occasion when I had the pleasure of talking with him. He was living then in the quaint old Temple, and I had brought some youthful enthusiasm to his feet. He listened with kindly attention —his curiously blond face, very long and solemn and white, like a dripping candle—and when I had finished he turned and said: "Charming of you, dear Le Gallienne! It's very charming—*but why not in a newspaper?*" Many a time since have I had occasion to recall that remark, with its shrewd human insight into that admiration, so vocal to one's face, and so oddly silent —in the newspapers.

Mr. Moore was then becoming known as one of the stormy petrels of the violent revolutionary age which was then coming upon us, and causing no little disquiet and anger in senior Victorian bosoms. Mr. William Archer, in the field of dramatic criticism, was another, and, of course, Mr. Bernard Shaw, with his Fabian socialism, his vegetarianism, his "pepper-and-salt" Jaeger woollen clothing, was still another. His plays were yet some way off. These men, with Mr. H. W. Massingham, the fighting editor of the radical *Daily Chronicle*, and one or two others constituted what was called "The New Journalism," marked by an aggressive, menacing individualism, a natural and often savage style of writing, which brought a peculiar freshness of atmosphere as of oncoming storm into the placid, conventional newspaper world.

It was immensely invigorating to hear men speaking out in a natural human voice, as it was startling to see actually in print audacities of opinion that gave us some such shock as Mr. Mencken has recently brought to America. One felt, too, that the New Journalism was grimly out for business, and there was an ominous rumbling in the air as of falling towers. But there was

a new "common" note, coarse and ill bred, in this
writing, too, sansculottish, so to say, which alone made
one feel that the world was passing out of the hands of
gentlemen—doubtless for its own good! One felt also
that these men, sincere and clever as they were, were of
a smaller race than the men of the great era that pre-
ceded them. There was a vulgar exploitation of minor
personalities. The era of the engineered boom was
beginning, and one had a feeling that men were getting
"famous" too quickly. The bud was already being
taken for the flower. Hasty unripe biographies began
to be written, and autobiography even was beginning
to precede achievement. Knighthoods, too, were already beginning to go cheap. For good or ill, the old
order was unmistakably changing. All the more, it was
a romantic age to be born in, for most of the great
figures of that old order were still alive, in embattled
eminence, or had but recently departed.

In politics Mr. Gladstone and Lord Beaconsfield
still loomed large, with the sinister figure of Mr.
Chamberlain for the protagonist of the new business-
man's government. In literature and art most of the
great Victorians were on their thrones: Ruskin at
Brantwood, Herbert Spencer in Brighton, Tennyson
rustling with laurels in Haslemere or the Isle of Wight
—as Andrew Lang wrote, "The Master's yonder in
the isle"—Carlyle was only nine years dead; most of
the pre-Raphaelites were still alive, and only eight
years before—that is before 1890—Rossetti still dwelt
in mysterious sacrosanct seclusion, like some high
priest behind the veil, in his old romantic house in
Chelsea ; Morris, with one foot in the new age, making
beautiful books at Kelmscott and selling tapestries and

wall-papers in Oxford Street, writing "The Dream of John Ball," and preaching socialism to unsympathetic mobs in Trafalgar Square; Swinburne and Theodore Watts (soon to change his name to Watts-Dunton) were keeping their odd bachelor household together in Putney; Meredith was in haughty rustication at Box Hill in Surrey; Browning, democratically ubiquitous at tea-parties and an indefatigable diner-out, was writing more and more cryptically, with occasional divine lyrical simplicities; and Matthew Arnold, as late as 1888, was still preaching "sweetness and light" to a world of Philistines. Cardinal Newman's beautiful fading figure was still at the Edgbaston Oratory, and the astute, worldly Cardinal Manning was still at Westminster. Painters such as Watts, Burne-Jones, and Millais were still painting; Henry Irving and the ever lovely Miss Ellen Terry were playing in that high temple of the drama, The Lyceum Theatre; Gilbert and Sullivan, with their imperishable operas, were delighting the town. The Gaiety Theatre, home of coryphées and gilded youth, was also in its apogee; while Wagner was the storm centre of serious music. Mrs. Langtry—Anadyomene, recently risen from the foam near Jersey —was the reigning beauty

A wonderful London! Illustrious presences, now rapidly becoming mythological, walked the streets, visible Immortals, and still I recall the thrill of seeing Henry Irving boarding a hansom in the Strand—for, with the one exception of Doctor Holmes, it was my first sight of a great man. Irving was the idol of London cabmen, and I remember the face of the cabby that drove him that day almost as clearly as his own—how it lit up at the sight of him, with what alacrity he climbed down from his box, with what pride and eager recognition of his celebrated fare he touched his hat and flung open the apron—"Mr. Hirving, sir!"—for he was not yet "Sir 'Enery." No prince of the blood could have received greater homage, and there was probably no cabman between the Lyceum and Charing Cross with whom Irving was not on friendly terms. There is a story that one evening, as Irving arrived at his stage door, the cab horse fell down dead. Laconically, Irving drew a twenty-pound note from his pocket, handed it to the cabby with "Buy another!", and vanished into the theatre.

To have seen Irving on the street seemed wonderful, but the sympathetic reader will doubtless understand my youthful feelings when, a few months afterwards, I sat at supper at Sir Arthur Pinero's and saw my hero within a few yards of me, and other great persons scattered about in careless profusion. "How those gods look!" But the climax of that unforgettable evening was when, having taken leave of my host and hostess, I was seeking my hat and coat in the cloakroom, a footman came running after me with "Wait a moment, sir. Mr. Irving would like to speak to you!" And there in the hall, for several incredible moments, he was walking to and fro by my side, with his hand in a brotherly way on my shoulder, and graciously pretending familiarity with my then not very voluminous writings. That strange, distinguished face, that even stranger voice, the voice of Hamlet and Shylock. . . . Could it be real? And then, a few days later, a letter in his handwriting, so cryptically undecipherable that I can reproduce it for the reader, who may care to see it, for the handwriting's sake, without much fear of his discovering its complimentary nature.

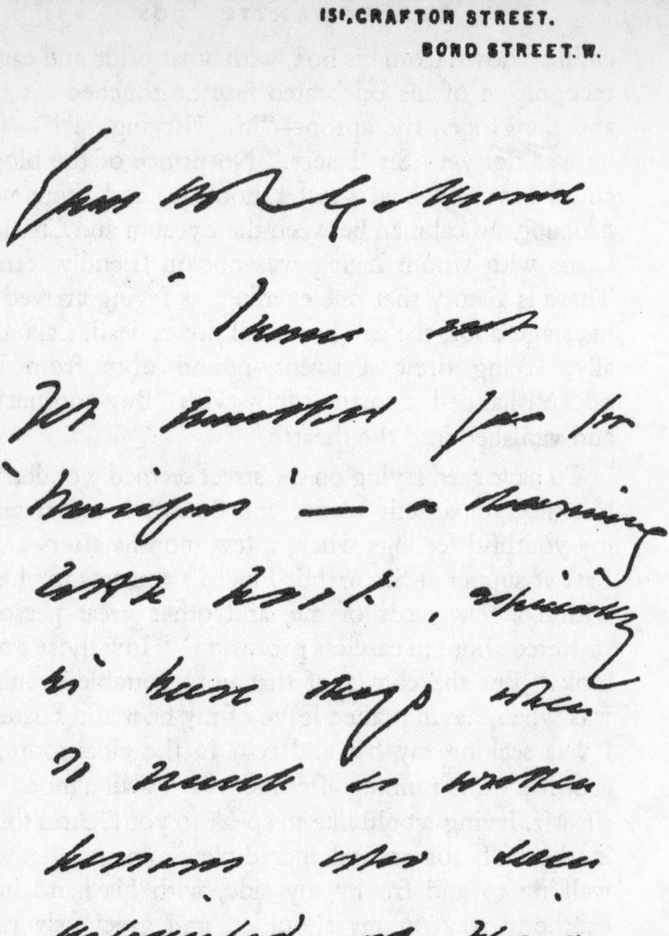

[handwritten letter, largely illegible]

... 'reviews' — a charming little book, especially ... is here they ... is much is written ...

Letter from Henry Irving
to Richard Le Gallienne

6 April 1895

It was to another famous actor of the time, Wilson Barrett—of "Claudian" and "Silver King" fame—that I owed, in Hazlitt's phrase, "My First Acquaintance with Poets." Mr. Barrett had engaged me as his "literary secretary," a post which entailed duties little more arduous than hanging about the wings—another wonder-world!—casting sheep's eyes on pretty young actresses waiting to go on. Mr. Barrett, having learned that I should like to meet Swinburne, offered to take me with him to the sacred "Pines, Putney" for lunch. Some few years before, as I have said, I had wondered if poets still existed in our modern prosaic world. Now I was to see one of the greatest living poets, actually living and breathing before me. "Ah, did you once see Shelley plain?" Well, I was going to see Swinburne, and so strange and dreamlike it seemed to me, that, when at last I found myself seated at luncheon, with the great lyric Master before me, I pinched my leg under the table to persuade myself of the reality of my experience. "There sits the poet of 'Atalanta in Calydon'," I said over and over to myself, as I watched him tenderly wiping with his napkin the neck of the pint of Bass which was Mr. Watts-Dunton's allowance to the friend over whose hazardously lyrical nature he watched with brotherly care.

I was all hush and awe that day, and any sense of humour I possessed was subdued by reverence. Though I did contrive on later visits to have one or two conversations with Swinburne, there was no question of my talking to him that day. To gaze on his splendid brow, still scantily aureoled with his flamboyant red hair, and lit up with eager blue eyes of a surprising youthfulness, was more than enough.

Besides, conversation with Swinburne was, generally speaking, impossible, for he was so impenetrably deaf that only the slightly raised utterance of Mr. Watts-Dunton, to which he was accustomed, or the most miraculous organ of Mr. Barrett's splendid voice, was able to pierce his aural solitude. When he entered the room he greeted me with that distinguished courtesy of manner which all who met him have observed, a courtly bow after the fashion of the great old world. That was all, but how much it seemed, and, even had he been able to hear me, I was too busy hero-worshipping to have found a word to say. He himself talked much and well, in a rather high voice, with a curious explosive, breathless, sing-song intonation, with something of impatient scorn, the subject being contemporary politics, and a curious, as it seemed to me, humourless humour, as of one to whom humour is inappropriate.

There was, indeed—I say it with unabated reverence —something absurd, as it were misbegotten, about Swinburne, which no truthful picture can omit; something that made people turn and laugh at him in the streets, as I once saw some carters do as he went by on Wimbledon Common, with his eccentric dancing, one might even say epileptic, gait, his palms spread open behind him in a tense nervous way. He was certainly an odd, scarcely human figure, and he and Watts-Dunton made the quaintest pair.

There is no harm, I hope, in setting down the humorous memory I have of a later visit at "The Pines," for surely one may smile at a great man's oddities without sacrilege, and in Watts-Dunton's case my admiration soon grew, as did that of all who knew

him, into genuine affection. No more generous friend
ever lived, and his kindness to young writers was a rare
and precious thing. On the day I am thinking of, the
peculiarities of these elderly Damon and Pythias seem
to have struck me with peculiar force, though, believe
me, I remained as conscious as ever that I was, so to
say, "in the Presence." I was to lunch with the two
great men alone, and I was far from unaware of the
honour. Still, as Swinburne entered the room, and
greeted me once more with that beautiful courtesy, I
was impressed as never before by the peculiarities of
his figure. He was a rather short man, with incredibly
narrow "champagne" shoulders, a disproportionately
long and slightly exuberant trunk, and short tripping
legs. His splendid head seemed far too big for his body
and gave him the appearance of one of those caricatures
in which a fantastically large head is placed on a
diminutive figure. His head, too, lolled to one side, as
if too heavy to carry, and the lower part of his face was
disastrously unfinished, almost chinless, and from the
wrinkles of his rather disagreeably inadequate chin
grew out a scant beard of thinly scattered hairs. As a
compensating feature, a large, commanding, aristo-
cratic nose must not be omitted. Seated at the table, he
continually jerked his body in a nervous way, and his
hands "twittered" before him in an uncomfortably
weird manner.

He had come to the table waving a copy of the
Saint James's Gazette with considerable excitement,
even irascibility. Something he had been reading had
evidently roused his indignation. It was a review of a
new poet, for whom he expressed a true Swinburnian,
polysyllabic scorn. He read aloud to us some extracts,

with his high, singing voice, breathing hard and spasmodically; and, catching sight of the paper afterwards, I noticed that he had written in French on the margins remarks of a highly objurgatory nature. The poet, I regret to add, was Francis Thompson. I kept to myself the fact that, as Mr. John Lane's reader, I was responsible for the publication of the offending poems! I forget what Mr. Watts-Dunton had to say by way of soothing agreement and mild rebuttal; and I remember better the conclusion of the lunch, which struck me as delightfully funny, though I rather despair of conveying the fun of it to the reader.

Mr. Watts-Dunton was seated at the head of the table and did the carving, Mr. Swinburne on his right and myself on his left. Mr. Watts-Dunton was a tiny man whose careless clothes always seemed too big for him. His face was as small as Swinburne's was large, a good brow with keen kindly eyes, and a long rat-like, or I had better say Mongolian, moustache. I have remarked on Mr. Swinburne's impenetrable deafness. Now Watts-Dunton also was deaf, deaf enough for all practical purposes. He was also very near-sighted, so that when a dish was put before him he had to bend his head close down over it, scanning it as near-sighted people scan small print. Well, at the end of the meal, the maid who waited upon us placed before him one of those tarts with criss-cross "open-work" pastry through which the jam of which it was composed was plainly visible, the colour of it unmistakable.

Bending over it, and scanning it as though it were some obscure Greek text, Mr. Watts-Dunton turned to Mr. Swinburne, and, with that ceremonious address which they always observed one towards the other, he called out in a loud voice:

"Mr. Swinburne, this is your favourite tart—black currant."

Thereupon the maid touched Mr. Watts-Dunton on the shoulder, and, shouting loudly to him in her turn, she said:

"Mr. Watts-Dunton, it's not black currant"—then louder still, "it's GREENGAGE."

Perhaps the reader may not see much to laugh at, but to me it seemed irresistibly comic, and, had the reader been there, I think he would have found it as hard to keep his face straight as I did.

Lunch being over, Mr. Swinburne invited me upstairs to his study to inspect the collection of rare quartos of the Elizabethan dramatists which was the apple of his eye: Ford, Webster, Dekker, and the rest; and it was my happiness and honour that day to add to that cherished collection a very scarce quarto of an obscure play by Thomas Kyd, "Soliman and Perseda." I had picked it up for five shillings. Such finds were possible to short purses in those days. I had brought it as appropriate tribute to the altar of the Master, but I had great difficulty in persuading him to accept it, for, of course, he knew its value. When, however, I had overcome his courteous scruples, the boyish pleasure he showed in his new acquisition, I might say toy, was exhilarating to see. That eager boyishness, which, even as an old man, he never lost, was one of the most charming and remarkable of his characteristics. His blue eyes seemed suddenly to flower in his face, and his whole countenance became so irradiated with interior light that one seemed to see the welling up of that deep lyric fount from which the most impassioned song in the English language had come. Certainly that afternoon I saw Shelley plain, saw the white fire that burns in a great poet's heart, and realized what it means to be "inspired" like the poets of old. All the absurdity on which I hope I have not laid too much stress disappeared in that strange transfiguring light, which grew even brighter as he read to me, or rather chanted, with intense excitement some scenes from the play on which he was then engaged, "The Duke of Gandia." How he revelled, with an utter absorbed unconsciousness, in the glory of the streaming jewelled words, evidently forgetting they were his own, loving them just for their own sake. He ended by lifting me into the seventh heaven by promising to give me the manuscript, when it was completed—a promise which I value none the less because it was unfulfilled. By this time he had grown more accustomed to my voice, so that we were able really to talk together, on a subject, too, which was peculiarly his own. I had remarked how little of romantic passion, as distinct from mere eroticism, there was in English poetry. He kindled at once at the theme, and together we went over the names of one English poet after another, ending by rejecting all but a very few, chief among which were Marlowe and Donne and Keats. Even Shakespeare he considered inadequate in that particular quality, in which, needless to say, Swinburne himself stands pre-eminent. French poetry, he agreed, was even poorer than English in that respect. To talk with Swinburne on passion in poetry was indeed a wonderful experience, and I regret that I took no notes of his glowing talk, and that it now remains but a vague glory in my memory.

From Swinburne's study I descended to Watts-

Dunton's, and he talked to me, in his familiar, discursive, *déshabillé* fashion, of Rossetti, whose most intimate friend he had been, while around us on the walls dreamed those strangely lovely faces Rossetti had made his own, drawings and paintings from Rossetti's own hand; and, dominating all, an immense cabinet of black oak, with decorative panels also by Rossetti, making a romantic contrast with the otherwise prim and commonplace atmosphere of the mid-Victorian room, suggestive of antimacassars and horsehair furniture. As the afternoon light faded, and the dream-faces glimmered in the dusk about us, Watts-Dunton talked of the life of Rossetti, which he was always writing, but which his easy-going indolence never allowed him to write. Rossetti had already been dead for several years, but the book never seemed to get any nearer. Two biographies, indeed, had long since appeared, and so promptly after Rossetti's funeral that Oscar Wilde, whose epigrams were already ruling London dinner tables, once said to me: "Whenever a great man dies, Hall Caine and William Sharp go in with the undertakers."

The last time I saw Swinburne he did not see me, and perhaps it is telling tales out of school to recall the occasion. Still, as I consider the reminiscence far from derogatory to him, and believe, too, that the reader will regard it with me as presenting him in a brotherly human aspect, I will hazard it. Swinburne, like some other poets of the time, Tennyson and Meredith for instance, was a great walker. Putney lies at the foot of Wimbledon Common, and it was Swinburne's custom to walk every morning from his house to the top of the common and back. It chanced that one morning I had been out early bicycling, and I had stepped into a shop at the top end of the Common to buy a newspaper. Whom should I come against, leaving as I was entering, but Swinburne? He did not see me, and I had no thought of disturbing his morning meditations. But when I came out of the shop I saw him ahead of me on his way home. It was then I noticed his fantastic manner of walking and heard those profane carters laughing at the great man of whom they knew nothing. As I watched him dancing oddly on his way, a profane idea struck me also. I remembered that there was at the head of the Common, a short distance away, an old inn called the Rose and Crown; I have referred to that bottle of Bass which was all that the protective Watts-Dunton, ever thoughtful of his well-being, considered good for him. Swinburne, needless to say, was no ordinary drunkard, but for him, as for so many other poets, strong drink was a mocker, and for him, with his orgiastic temperament, it was more potent and dangerous than for less sensitive men. Thus, as I remembered the Rose and Crown, I could not help wondering if, now that he was out of the clutches of his friend, he might not be inclined to a little human truancy. So I hung behind till the inn came in sight. "Will he pass it?" I smiled to myself, or "Will he go in?" I was not left in doubt, for, as a billiard ball glides into the pocket, the author of "Atalanta in Calydon" suddenly disappeared. There was no one but me and the carters to see. I smiled to think of Watts-Dunton at the bottom of the hill, and, after waiting a few moments, I myself entered the inn. It was one of those old inns in which the tap-room is partitioned off into various cosy sections. I glanced into one and another

of them, but there was no sign of my illustrious friend.
Perhaps I had been mistaken, after all. Then, leaning
on the bar, I ordered my own "morning," as Pepys
would say, from the gay young barmaid, and presently brought our conversation round to the gentleman who had entered before me, remarking that I was
acquainted with him, and wondered what had become
of him. "Oh," she replied, "the gentleman" never
drank at the bar, but every morning, at the same hour,
he dropped in and, repairing to a private room,
punctually consumed a bottle of Burgundy, alone with
his thoughts. Needless to say, he did not fall in my
estimation on that account. On the contrary, it but
made him the more comradely human, and I rejoiced,
too, that, in spite of his friendly gaoler, the poet did
contrive thus to warm his veins with that generous
ichor. I waited around on the grass outside for perhaps three-quarters of an hour, and then suddenly
again there was the divine "Algy" once more on his
homeward way, apparently none the worse for his
truant libation.

I have said that I "commenced author" with a book
on George Meredith. To-day it seems to me a very
youthful performance, as is perhaps not surprising,
for I was very young when I wrote it, too young probably to tackle so difficult a master. However, I am
proud to have had the assurance that it served its
purpose of introducing so great a writer to many who
at that time had scarcely heard his name. For his poetry
in particular, then unknown except to that "acute and
honourable minority" to whom he addressed it, I am
glad to think that it did some missionary service, as
Meredith himself graciously and generously acknow-

ledged. I mention these details because it was that little book which won me the friendship of perhaps the greatest personality, as certainly the greatest intellectual and spiritual influence, of the time. George Meredith is one of the most conspicuous instances of deferred recognition in literature. For years "Richard Feverel" and "The Egoist" found an audience "fit" indeed but pitiably "few," and for more than thirty years the creator of such masterpieces was constrained to plod along as a publisher's reader, for a paltry two hundred pounds a year. This neglect, borne with philosophic courage not unmixed with scorn, was not, however, without its embittering effect, so that, when recognition did come, Meredith had grown haughtily indifferent to it. The neglect of his poetry was a matter on which he was particularly sensitive, as an extract from one of his letters to me will show. I had asked his permission to include some of his poems in an anthology for which I was doing some work. Here is his answer:

BOX HILL,
December 22, 1891.

DEAR MR. LE GALLIENNE,

It is an old apology for unhappy refusals, but true, that I would concede to you what for no other, if my objection were not invincible. I have declined many invitations of the sort, and I cannot give way in this instance. I have not really a place in the Anthology; it would confound the public to see me in that midst, and as I dislike mere collections, why should this other annoyance be added to the list attending my silly publications of verse—poetical matter, not poems, as it has been said. Your "Narcissus" gave me very great pleasure indeed. It is as richly garrulous as a May black-bird, limpid as a brook, promising masterpieces in the rarest style of essay. If your wife would honour us with her company some day in February, I should much like to welcome you both for a night, that we may converse.

Very truly,
GEORGE MEREDITH.

In another letter he has a similar reference to his novels, as well as an affectionate reference to Robert Louis Stevenson, who was one of the earliest of his disciples:

BOX HILL, DORKING.
DEC. 21, '94.

DEAR MR. LE GALLIENNE,

If you should be disposed to come to me the first week of January, you will be warmly welcomed, and you will help to animate me at least. Whether I shall make the return for it, I can't foresee. I have just concluded a novel, likely to share the fate of my others with the reviewers, but the latter part has worn me—owing to my state of health more than the task. I trust that the report of Louis Stevenson's death may be untrue. It is I who should go, not he, who is young and loved. The signs of the love are pleasant.

Your faithful
GEORGE MEREDITH.

At this time locomotor ataxia was beginning to threaten him, as his handwriting gave evidence,

and soon he, the mighty walker, who loved especially
to walk in the rain of a south-west wind, was to
resign himself to a Bath chair. When I first knew
him, however, he was still actively on his feet. His
pretty cottage in one of the most beautiful parts of
Surrey was perhaps the most famous place of pil-
grimage in the '90s. There every week-end some of the
finest spirits and brightest intellects of the day used
to gather to do him homage. It was, therefore, with
no little trepidation that I, too, received the royal
invitation, one amazing morning, to repair thither for
my "accolade."

Meredith was rather an overwhelming personality,
particularly for diffident youth. A brilliant and fantastic
talker, one needed to be nearer his age and more his
intellectual match to follow him through his dazzling
verbal swordplay and whimsical soliloquies. But me
he received with quite a fatherly sympathy and soon
put me at my ease, though, as his talk was exactly
like his books, elaborately fanciful, yet knotted with
thought, a thicket of thorn-bushes hung with sudden
starry blossoms, one had to snatch at what one could,
magnetized by the rush and verve of his resonant
voice, and dominated by his lordly manner. It was a
manner, it seemed to me, slightly theatrical, almost
affectedly bravura, and made one think that he must
be very like his own Roy Richmond. I reflected, too,
that Ulysses must have been such a man, a tall, lean,
rugged fighter, with that far-wandered crafty look in a
face that seemed to me characteristically Welsh,
roughly bearded, high-browed, with keen grey eyes
and slightly up-turned fighting nose. An immense
intellectual alertness that seemed to pervade all his

vigorous frame was his most characteristic expression. His portrait by Hollyer, now known to everyone who reads, is exactly himself.

Meredith's talk, as I have hinted, was largely of the nature of fantasia. Epigrammatist as he was in his writings, it contained little detachable epigram, being in this respect entirely the opposite of the elaborately built talk of Oscar Wilde, of whom I shall have to speak later. Therefore it was difficult to remember. It was like an impromptu played by some great violinist, of which one can carry away little more than the general effect. Thus I can but dimly indicate it by a fragment or two which I recall from the dinner table that first evening. There were several other guests present, including Mr. John Lane, who was one of the earliest and most enthusiastic Meredithians, and to whom my little book owed an elaborate bibliography which I now regard as its most valuable part. Seated at the table, too, were Mr. Meredith's beautiful young daughter, who then kept house for him in his widowhood, and his son, really a very modest and wholesome young Englishman, whom he had a rather cruel way of teasing and addressed as the "Sagamore." With a kingly wave of his hand towards him, he would say: "Behold the Sagamore! Mark that lofty brow! Stand in awe with me before the wisdom that sits there enthroned . . ." and so he would proceed mercilessly to improvise on the sublime serenity of Wise Youth, seated there so confidently at the top of the world, till the poor tortured Sagamore would blush to the roots of his hair. I myself, on another occasion, was to experience a touch of the lash of that relentless mocking tongue, as I will tell later.

Meredith was somewhat of a connoisseur of wine and prided himself on his small but choice cellar. I forget what the particular wine was that we drank that evening, but the fact that one bottle had been finished and stood empty at Meredith's right hand gave him an opportunity for a characteristic fantasia, of which unfortunately I can remember but the bare theme. Waving towards the bottle with a magnificent gesture, he addressed the maid who waited on us, and who, being, of course, familiar with her master's eccentric eloquence, broke at once into expectant smiles.

"Mary," he said, "you behold here a body from which the soul is departed. A body without a soul! Mark it there empty and useless, of no value to gods or men! Once full of genial fire, golden warmth for heart and brain, alive with inspiring ichor, the Hymettian fount of noble talk and soaring thought, the *elixir vitæ* of wit, making of man's dull brain a thing of magic and dreams, lifting our dull mortality into the highest heaven of invention! But behold it now, a hollow echoing shell, a forlorn cadaver, its divine life all poured out of it, no laughter in it, no wisdom, no human kindness in it, any more for ever. What shall be done with it, Mary? A body from which the soul is departed! What do we with such? What is there to be done, but to hurry it out of sight of gods and men— mournful reminder of feasts that are at an end, and dimming candles. . . ."

Not all these were his actual words, but such was the gist of them, such his way of playing with an idea. And so for some minutes he went on, piling fancy on fancy, till, with a final gesture of dismissal, he concluded with "Mary! remove this bottle!"

On another occasion when I visited him, he took me with him up the hill that rose behind his house, where stood a little châlet of two rooms picturesquely situated under the lee of some woodland. Here he did his writing. The room was furnished mainly with bookshelves, chiefly filled, I noticed, with French and German authors. And here, for an unforgettable hour or two, he read me some chapters of "The Amazing Marriage," and his latest poem, "The Empty Purse," one of the most difficult of his writings, and hard to follow even in print. As he read, sonorously and rapidly, with an eye alert for intelligent comprehension in his listener, it was a scrambling business to follow its drift, but I contrived, I hope, to make some show of grasping it, and to make some comments not too hopelessly astray. Of course, the wonderful thing was that the novelist who wrote of Lucy and Richard by the river and the poet of "Love in the Valley" should be actually reading to me at all. It was almost like listening to Shakespeare reading "Hamlet."

As we strolled down to the house once more, I took courage to ask him if some day he could spare me a piece of his manuscript, a request to which he gave a ready assent. The manuscripts of several of his novels, by the way, he left as a bequest to his gardener, to whom they proved a valuable legacy.

Lunch was afoot when we entered the house and I was to leave by the afternoon train. Two ladies, poets who collaborated under the name of "Michael Field," were my fellow guests on this occasion, and I still remember with gratitude their pleas on my behalf in the little scene that followed. We were nearing the end of the meal, and, keeping Meredith's promise of a page of his manuscript in mind, I ventured to remind him of it, and with well-meant diffidence, I said: "Of course, Mr. Meredith, I don't expect anything important, I don't expect—I don't expect—the manuscript of 'The Egoist' or 'Richard Feverel' "—and then, in an evil moment, I added, "only a little poem."

The ignominy of the moment is with me yet. Immediately I realized how tragically I had put my foot in it. The air seemed to grow still as with imminent thunder, and then, with merciless sarcasm, he let loose his lightnings upon me.

"Oh, I see," he said, turning to my fellow guests. "Mark you that! He wants nothing important. Only a little poem! How truly, after all, he speaks. Everyone knows the unimportance of my poor poems—'poetical matter, not poems' as some person of insight has acutely said. Yes! nothing important—only a little poem!"

So he went on, while I expostulated in vain, humbled in the dust. The two kindly ladies came staunchly to my rescue, but the damage was done. There was no mending the matter that day—and I never got my manuscript.

So I tasted the whip of his cruel tongue—all the more cruel, I could not help reflecting, because I had, as he well knew, done my small best to champion those very poems he accused me of belittling. But after all, it was only a rather pathetic sign of how deep the iron of unappreciation had entered into his soul. Nowadays one may somewhat doubtfully wonder whether he would be pleased to find that his poems are read more than his novels, which probably "Modern Love" and "Love in the Valley" will long outlive.

On my next visit to Box Hill, Meredith received me with his usual kindness, but, needless to say, I never revived the subject of my "little poem"! On that occasion he was in a reminiscent vein and talked much of Tennyson, whom he admired as a poet, but of whose personality he had little good to say. He told me several anecdotes of his egotism and boorish manners which were highly amusing. Tennyson, like not a few of the *genus irritabile*, was inordinately sensitive to criticism. As was said of Byron, the praise of the greatest could not take the sting from the censure of the meanest. Meredith, when a comparatively young man, had visited him in his house at Haslemere, and, one morning after breakfast, had gone out walking with him across the downs. He had hoped, he confessed, that the great laurelled poet might take some friendly interest in the work he was doing (Meredith's own sympathy towards young writers was generous indeed), but no! By the mail that morning there had come some quite unimportant criticism by some quite unimportant person, and Tennyson could think of nothing else. Meredith described how, as they walked side by side, Tennyson's deep voice went booming along the hills: "Apollodorus says I'm not a great poet!" till Meredith got tired of it and ventured at last to express his surprise that Tennyson should consider the criticism of the insignificant Apollodorus worth thinking about. But it was no use, the deep voice continued to boom on: "Apollodorus says I'm not a great poet!" And that seems to have been all that Meredith got out of his visit.

A remarkable instance of the boorishness of Tennyson's manners relates also to this same super-sensitiveness to criticism. Tennyson, then Lord, and Lady Tennyson were guests at lunch in a certain great house where many distinguished people had been invited to meet them. All were gathered together in the drawing-room, chatting before lunch, Tennyson taking no part but prowling about the tables on which lay the new books of the day, picking up this one and that, ignoring his surroundings. As his hostess watched him, a sudden alarming thought came over her. There had just been published a famous book on Tennyson by the learned scholar Churton Collins, in which Collins had made a point of tracking down Tennyson's considerable indebtedness to the classics, quoting Tennyson and this and that Greek or Latin author in parallel passages. Instantly the hostess remembered that this offensive book was there on one of the tables. She had forgotten to remove it, and now in a panic she looked wildly around in the hope that it was not too late. But alas! Tennyson was already bending over that very table. As by instinct he had scented out the very book. It was already in his hand, and he was glaring at it with infuriated eyes. There was nothing to be done but to await the event, which was not long in coming. Presently, with a deep grunt of indignation, Tennyson turned to his wife and made for the door of the drawing room. "My dear," he boomed out, "I'm afraid we must be going"; and, actually, without a word of explanation or excuse—they went. Which, to adapt what I once heard Meredith say of a picnic ruined by sudden rain, as the drenched picnickers trailed back over the hill—"funeral of picnic!"—was decidedly the funeral of the poor lady's lunch. Next day she wrote to

Lady Tennyson regretting the incident. But still no apologies, and Lady Tennyson's only response was that it was indeed a distressing occurrence—and that Alfred had been ill in bed ever since.

Tennyson, while affecting to dread observation, was none the less no little vain, a weakness of which Meredith gave me this amusing illustration. Tennyson and William Morris were once walking together on a road in the Isle of Wight. Suddenly in the distance appeared two cyclists wheeling towards them. Tennyson immediately took alarm, and, turning to Morris, growled out, "Oh, Morris, what shall I do: those fellows are sure to bother me!" Thereupon Morris drew him protectively to his side. "Keep close to me," he said, "I'll see that they don't bother you." The cyclists came on, sped by without a sign, and presently disappeared on the horizon. There was a moment or two of silence, and then Tennyson, evidently huffed that he had attracted no attention, once more growled out, "They never even looked at me!"

Very likely Meredith, with his dramatic sense, heightened these stories somewhat, but there is little doubt that they were substantially true and characteristic; and I myself once heard a story from one who took part in it that completely confirms them.

At one time I rented a little cottage in Surrey, some five miles from Haslemere. My landlord, whose name was Ward, was a modest little man, a builder by trade, of some cultivation. He told me that, one summer, two ladies from the North of England had come to visit him and his wife, and, hearing that Tennyson's house was in the neighbourhood, expressed the wish to see it. Mr. Ward, knowing all the conditions, attempted to dissuade them. It was a very hot July day, he reminded them, and it was quite a long walk. Also Tennyson's house was invisible from the road, enshrouded in a girdle of pinewood. Besides, the gate was plastered with notice boards warning off strangers —not exactly "Visitors Will Be Shot," but words somewhat to that effect. The ladies, however, were persistent. Surely the great poet could not object to their looking at the outside of his house, et cetera. So Mr. Ward gave in, and they started out. After a long hot walk, they at length arrived at the gate, and Mr. Ward pointed out the minatory notice boards. They could see what they had to face! However, if they cared to take the risk, he was willing. So they pushed open the gate and proceeded along the winding carriage drive. But they had not gone very far, when two great hounds came padding round a curve, followed by the sound of two sticks on the gravel. Then suddenly round the corner appeared the bent figure of a vast old man, dressed in a great cloak and wide sombrero. They were in for it, and there was nothing for little Mr. Ward to do but face the music. Hat in hand, he approached the great man, who stopped short and sternly surveyed him from under the brim of his sombrero, with deep old weary eyes, like an old mastiff's. Humbly the little man explained that these ladies had meant no intrusion, that they were great admirers of his poetry, from the North Country, and, being in the neighbourhood, it had been their great desire just to look at the outside of the house where lived the poet who had written "Kind hearts are more than coronets," et cetera—that, of course, they had not dreamed of disturbing him, nothing more than just that. Meanwhile Tennyson continued to look him up and down, and presently rumbled in his great voice:

"Did you see the notice at the gate?"

Mr. Ward admitted that they had, but that they had hoped that under the circumstances . . . and Mr. Ward repeated what he had said before. For a long while Tennyson stood pondering, as though some great question of state hung in the balance, and then at length, with solemn shaking of his head, announced his decision:

"It can't be done!" he said, "it can't be done!" and waved them back towards the gate.

II

AT ANY given period of transition there are always three generations actively in being: the great old men on the heights in the background, still wielding authority from their achievement, and in some cases still achieving, the men in their fifties, sixties, seventies, and even eighties, in the full vigour of their maturity, occupying the middle distance, and the young men in the foreground dreaming and plotting the creation of the future. I have dealt with some of the great old men on the heights when I reached London around 1890. One or two others remain, notably Herbert Spencer. I never met that great philosopher, but friends of mine have told me stories of him at first hand of a highly characteristic and amusing nature. Mr. Spencer's intellectual greatness was accompanied by some eccentric personal traits which unavoidably lent themselves to somewhat irreverent anecdote. For example, whenever he paid a visit of any length to a friend, he sent ahead of his arrival a postcard on which he had written the details of the diet which his host was expected to provide for him. Grant Allen, who was one of his most devoted disciples, showed me several of these quaint postcards. I wish I had begged one from him for the benefit of the reader, but unhappily I failed in that foresight.

One of Mr. Spencer's most marked characteristics was his extreme impatience, not to say irascibility, in discussion. The smallest difference of opinion in the most deferential of his admirers would produce a state of irritation alarming to witness, threatening even, it used to be said, to the action of his heart. Therefore, for all conversational occasions he had equipped himself with a pair of ear-clips, which, so soon as any such danger-point was neared, he clapped on firmly, and thus immediately put an end to the discussion. Mr. Frederick Harrison, the well-known historian and "Positivist," once told me an illustrative story of which he himself was the innocent storm centre. In those days, Mr. Harrison, still a young man, was regarded as an advanced radical thinker, though I imagine he would seem no little of a conservative in our day, when we are all so inured to every variety of "redness." The occasion was one of those famous breakfasts given by George Henry Lewes, the husband of George Eliot. Mr. Harrison found himself seated between two formidable figures, no less than Tennyson on his left and Herbert Spencer on his right. He was not, I believe, acquainted with either of them, certainly not with Tennyson, though Tennyson evidently knew who he was, and it was from Tennyson that the first conversational advances came—somewhat in this fashion. Mr. Harrison had been for some moments aware that Tennyson was observing him with no friendly eye. He, however, affected not to notice it, but this was not to avail him; for presently the deep voice growled out:

"I suppose you know who I am?"

On which Mr. Harrison mildly avowed his ignorance—in itself, need one say, an unforgivable offence. After a thunderous pause, his gracious neighbour returned to the charge, with:

"I'm Mr. Tennyson, and if I thought as you do—*I'd go and hang myself!*" Such was Tennyson's idea of breakfast-table amenities.

I don't know what answer Mr. Harrison made, but being a first-class fighting man, it was probably spirited. So much for his neighbour on the left; but soon he is to become involved even more deeply with his neighbour on the right. Having started some philosophic subject with Herbert Spencer, he from time to time quite deferentially ventured to express opinions that were his own but not the philosopher's, innocently unobservant of the rising storm—which suddenly broke by Spencer clapping on his ear-clips and behaving as though on the verge of an epileptic fit. Whereupon the host Lewes, and another friend who knew Spencer's peculiarities, rushed to his side, and each taking an arm, raised him bodily from the chair, hurried him from the room, and thrust him into a hansom cab. When they came back Lewes turned vehemently on poor Harrison: "My dear Harrison," he said, "I thought you knew better than to contradict Spencer. You might have killed him!"

Another story of Spencer is of a more peaceful, even domestic nature. It takes us back to the time of the Boer War, and introduces, too, one of the most individual and romantic figures of the period, the poet and anti-Imperialist, Wilfrid Scawen Blunt. Both Blunt and Spencer, it is perhaps hardly necessary to say, were pro-Boers and therefore lonely men. Feeling the need of someone to talk to on the subject, Blunt went down to see Spencer at Brighton, where he lived in an atmosphere of embalmed mid-Victorianism, quite untempered, as in the case of Swinburne and Watts-Dunton, by pre-Raphaelitism. When Blunt arrived, he was ushered into an upper room and found the philosopher reclining on a horsehair sofa.

"You will excuse my not rising, Mr. Blunt," he said, placing his hand on his side with an explanatory gesture, "my heart . . ."

The two brother pro-Boers then fell to, denouncing the British Government and all its works, and so thorough and passionate was their agreement that Mr. Spencer's customary agitation overcame him, though this time it came from the opposite of the usual cause. To agree with Spencer evidently had its dangers also. But on this occasion no ear-clips were in requisition. Quite otherwise.

"Mr. Blunt, would you mind ringing that bell?" said Spencer. "There is a lady of my household who plays to me when my nerves grow over-excited."

Then, on the summons, there appeared a little timid spinster lady, clad in rusty black silk such as we associate with ancient umbrellas.

Without a word she sat down to an old-fashioned upright piano and tinkled on its antique strings, playing as David played before Saul; till at length the philosopher indicated that her soothing work had been accomplished, and she vanished silently as she had entered.

Shortly afterwards there was the sound from downstairs of another bell.

"That," Spencer explained, "is the luncheon bell. I regret, Mr. Blunt, that I cannot accompany you, for the little I eat I eat up here."

So Mr. Blunt repaired downstairs, meeting on the way a domestic carrying a tray loaded with smoking mutton-chops and other hearty viands which formed the philosopher's frugal meal.

Arriving at the luncheon table, Mr. Blunt found himself seated next to the little lady who had played the piano, and another dim little lady like unto her.

As conversation was not brisk, Mr. Blunt felt it incumbent on him to make a gallant attempt at sustaining it; so, turning to the two ladies, in his courtly manner, he said:

"I suppose you have lived with Mr. Spencer for many years?"

Perhaps the little faded black-silk ladies had humour —it almost seems as if they must have had—for, with a touch of spinster gaiety, they both rippled out together:

"Oh no, indeed! Mr. Spencer never keeps any of us for more than six months—for fear we should grow too attached to him!"

It is necessary perhaps to know Herbert Spencer's physiognomy to appreciate the full flavour of this remark.

In 1890 there were several other men of the race of giants still in the world, men of alarming tendencies, and belonging less to their own time than to the future they were forcefully shaping: Tolstoi in Russia, Zola in France, and Ibsen and Björnson in Norway. Owing to the activity of certain "advanced" publishers, translations of their strange "new" writings were filling the English atmosphere with portents of change, to the joy of the younger men and the misgivings of their elders. Zola was in his prime, and "Nana" was regarded as the superfluity of naughtiness. His courageous English publisher, Henry Vizetelly, served two terms in gaol for publishing him: six months, with a fine of one hundred pounds, for "La Terre" in 1888, and three months, with a fine of two hundred pounds, in 1889 for "Nana" and some others of his novels. England also had her own apostle of "naturalism" in Mr. Thomas Hardy, one of the giants happily still left us, the sensation caused by his publication of "Tess of D'Urbervilles" in 1891 and "Jude the Obscure" in 1895 being hard to realize to-day. But Ibsen was perhaps the figure of most sinister portent. Sir Edmund Gosse had begun translating him as far back as 1872, Mr. William Archer—whom knighthood also overcame just before his death—quickly seconding him; and the production of "Ghosts" and "Hedda Gabler" and "A Doll's House" were the thrilling, even terrifying, theatrical events of the time.

I had the good fortune to see and speak with Ibsen while on a visit to Norway, at which time I also spent some days with Björnson at his country home. I will tell of my stay with Björnson first. I had gone to Norway with some English journalists, and in Christiania had struck up a friendship with one of the younger writers of the day, Mr. Rosencrantz Johnson, who belonged to a group calling themselves the "Bohèmes," whose darling desire, like similar leagues of youth before and since, was to "*épater la bourgeoisie.*" Mr. Johnson was a friend of Bj rnson's and suggested our paying him a visit in company. Björnson lived near Lillehammer, in a pine-clad valley at the end of a beautiful lake, which we crossed in the early morning, arriving at Aulestad—Björnson's home—in one of those tiny buggies called carrioles, before breakfast-time. Aulestad was a big verandahed house on the side of a wooded slope, and as we climbed up to it, there was our host, with his leonine head and great shaggy white hair, awaiting us, his arms stretched out in welcome, like a patriarch—though as a matter of fact he was little beyond sixty. He was an impressive figure of a man, with his broad sturdy shoulders, his eyes and nose like an eagle's—half lion, half eagle, so to say—suggesting immense strength and magnetic force. He seemed indeed like a hero from the old Scandinavian sagas come to life again, and, as he embraced us, we felt swept up into a larger, keener air. We noticed that he carried a bath towel over his shoulder, which he immediately explained.

"I am off for my bath in the woods," he said, "will you join me?" He spoke English, I may say, like an Englishman.

It was an heroic welcome, but we were game, and presently the three of us were tramping through the woods till we came to where a mountain stream fell in a torrent of white water down the face of a rock. Planks had been placed at the foot of the fall. "This is my shower bath," said Björnson, as he stripped, and there presently he stood, firm as a rock, beneath the cataract, the water pouring over his strong shoulders, his white head white as the foam, and shouting with joy of the morning. So might some great old water-god have stood and laughed amid the sun-flashing spray. It was a picture of elemental energy never to be forgotten, and, as one watched him there, one could well understand the power that made him the uncrowned king of his country.

Then, nothing loath, we repaired to the house for breakfast, and here again all was "saga," and one seemed to be seated in the hall of Sigurd the Volsung; for the master of the house and his lady, beautiful and commanding like her lord, sat at the end of a long table, royally side by side, on a slightly raised dais, with my friend and me, their guests, to right and left of them. One expected an aged harper to appear at any moment. Below us sat Björnson's daughter, Bergliot, named after his greatest poem, a glorious girl made out of gold and the blue sky, with whom, married men though we were, Johnson and I at once fell hopelessly in love. The tall brothers of the old ballads were not lacking, and other members of the household lined the table. The breakfast, too, belonged to "saga"—no shredded wheat and glass-of-milk business, but the robust Norwegian breakfast of heroes, roast meats and pungently spiced and smoked fishes, and, if not exactly horns of mead, bumpers of ale and *apéritifs* of schnapps. But, before we ate anything, there was a ceremony to be performed. Björnson rose and, making us welcome in one of his eloquent speeches, he bade the company drink *skaal* to his guests, which was promptly done with a noble heartiness. Mrs. Björnson had inquired about my wife, why she was not with me, and so forth.

"But you have her photograph in your pocket," added the poet, "out with it!" So the photograph being produced, Björnson held it up to the company, and once more bade them drink *skaal* to the absent English lady.

It was a gloriously different world from London, a dream out of a book of Norse fairy tales, romantically unreal, yet how invigoratingly human, with what a gusto in living!

We spent several days with the great Norseman, and

I had many talks with him, pacing to and fro in his library, his hand, father-like, on my shoulder. We talked much of English literature, in which, of course, he was well read, and he inquired if I knew his great English friends Mr. Gosse and Mr. Archer, a respectful acquaintance with whom I was happy to acknowledge. But at that time his heart was more occupied with the politics of his country than with literature, as he was engaged just then in his famous patriotic struggle to separate Norway from Sweden, in which, of course, he eventually succeeded. As everyone knows, he was a great orator, with a voice that carried across huge crowds in the open air. I never heard him under such conditions, but I shall never forget his radiant, impassioned eloquence as I walked to and fro by his side in that Aulestad study. Once—as with Meredith, though not so disastrously—I came near to putting my foot in it. It was a terrible thing to do, but he generously forgave me, for I was a stranger and naturally didn't know better. I mentioned the name of Ibsen! Then, indeed, he looked like an old lion. He stopped short, fire in his eyes and nostrils, and, shaking his great white mane, he thundered out: "IBSEN!"

A pause, and then again, with withering contempt, "Ibsen is not a man—he is only *a pen!*"

I knew nothing then of the bitter rivalry between the two great men, nor I suppose had Björnson, at that time, any inkling of the ironic stroke Fate was soon to deal to him, for whom should that beautiful Bergliot of his come afterwards to marry but Ibsen's son—Sigurd Ibsen! The marriage was probably no more to the taste of one father than of the other, and I

have heard since that when, the young people sticking
to their guns, the ceremony became inevitable, infinite
management of the reluctant fathers was necessary to
prevent an explosion. Both were present at the church,
but, in ordering the arrangement, the dangerous
question arose, which was to precede the other in the
bridal procession. At last some diplomatist struck on a
happy compromise, and the two fiery Norsemen
walked side by side, if not arm in arm.

When the time came to say good-bye, it was this
golden bride of Sigurd who was to drive us in a sort
of wagonette to the lake ferry. Several of us were
going, but there was only room for one of us by the
beautiful Bergliot's side on the box. Naturally, there
was a fierce rivalry for the coveted seat, and it makes
me happy to this day to remember that it was me that
she chose! We couldn't speak a word to each other,
but there are situations that are happy enough without
words. So once more in the early morning, Björnson
again with arms outstretched, in valedictory blessing,
"flags flying in town and harbour," we went off
laughing into the sunlight. Again I had seen Shelley
plain, and I have few memories that I cherish more
than those days at Aulestad with its great-hearted host
and hostess, not to speak of their fairy-tale daughter,
by whose side I drove off that light-hearted morning,
while I hugged close under my arm a copy of "The
Heritage of the Kurts" which Björnson had given me
for remembrance.

Back in Christiania, my friend with the name from
"Hamlet" announced that on the morrow we must
see Ibsen, not indeed, *en famille*, for he knew him but
slightly, but as all Christiania could see him every day,

if so minded, as he lunched in regal taciturnity at the
Grand Café, with clock-work precision at one. It would
be little more than the cat looking at the king, he
explained, for Ibsen was not Björnson, and his heart
was anywhere but on his sleeve. We were there in
good time, for, said my friend, "you must not miss his
entrance."

The large café was crowded, but we found a good
table on the aisle, not far from the door. We had not
long to wait, for, punctually on the stroke of one,
there entering the doorway was the dour and bristling
presence known to all the world in caricature—
caricatures which were no exaggeration, but, as in the
case of Swinburne, just the man himself. The great
ruff of white whisker, ferociously standing out all
round his sallow, bilious face, as if dangerously
charged with electricity, the immaculate silk hat, the
white tie, the frock-coated martinet's figure, dressed
from top to toe in old-fashioned black broadcloth, at
once funereal and professorial, the trousers concer-
tinaed, apparently with dandiacal design, at the ankles,
over his highly polished boots, the carefully folded
umbrella, all was there apparitionally visible before
me: a forbidding, disgruntled, tight-lipped presence,
starchily dignified, straight as a ramrod: there he was,
with a touch, as I hinted, of grim dandyism about him,
but with no touch of human kindness about his parch-
ment skin, or small, fierce badger eyes. He might have
been a Scotch elder entering the kirk. As he entered,
and proceeded with precisian tread to the table reserved in perpetuity for him, and which no one else
would have dreamed of occupying, a thing new and
delightful—to me a mere Anglo-Saxon—suddenly

happened. As one man, the whole café was on its feet in an attitude of salute, and a stranger standing near me who evidently spoke English and recognized my nationality said to me in a loud but reverent aside, "That is our great poet—Henrik Ibsen." All remained standing till he had taken his seat, as in the presence of a king, and I marvelled joyously at a people that thus did homage to their great men, not without reflections on the Anglo-Saxon's very different attitude towards its great. I thought, suppose it were Swinburne, or even Tennyson, entering the Café Royal—how forlornly anonymous would be their luncheon, with probably scarcely a soul in the place knowing enough about them to do them reverence. Certainly it is worth while to be a great man in a little country, and it must be inspiring to him thus to hear about him such "rustle of the loved Apollian leaves."

My friend Rosencrantz insisted that I must be taken to the great man's table to pay my respects, though I begged to be let off. Why should I intrude on the Presence? Besides, what could I find to say?

"You need have no fear of conversation," said my friend, "for Ibsen speaks nothing but Norwegian and Italian, and I presume you speak neither."

As I reluctantly gave in and approached the great man, on whom a reverential waiter was in attendance, Rosencrantz whispered to me: "Tell him—I'll translate for you—tell him that all the English women adore him. That will be enough. You'll see!"

So I was presented as a young English writer, and I must say very graciously received. Then, at a nudge from Rosencrantz, I got off my little speech, which my friend duly translated. He was right—instantly the dour face lit up with something like a smile of gratified vanity, and he nodded acknowledgments with a dry twinkle deep in his ambushed eyes. The little banality had evidently pleased him, and he turned to Rosencrantz with a question to translate to me: "Did I know Miss Robins?"—Miss Robins being the first actress to interpret his plays on the English stage.

Perhaps I need hardly say that I left unmentioned our recent visit to Björnson—whose remark I recalled to myself as I observed the fiercely hirsute envelope of that keen ironic mind, thinking, too, that strangely housed there was also the great poet of "Brand" and "Peer Gynt."

"Ibsen is not a man, he is only a pen!" Ah! dear Herr Björnson—but what a pen!

To return to London, in what I have called the middle distance between the great old men on the heights and the young men in the foreground, there were several distinguished figures who were already half immortals, men in the process of literary deification, though as yet, some of them, vigorously achieving, and visible socially at clubs and dinner parties like other ordinary mortals. One of the elder of these, and of the most entirely charming among the personalities of the time, was Frederick Locker, later known as Locker-Lampson, whose "London Lyrics" was already a classic of *vers de société*; a fascinating blend of man-about-town—with a marked suggestion of French elegance and *esprit*—country gentleman, poet, *raconteur*, and virtuoso, at once delicately ironical and gentle in manner, and wholly tender hearted. Perhaps he is better known to-day by his famous library, for he was one of the great book-collectors, and the catalogue

which he made of his books under the title of "The
Rowfant Library" is a bibliographical classic. But it is
as a poet that he will survive among the small but
distinguished band which includes Praed, Calverley,
Hood, Oliver Wendell Holmes, and Austin Dobson.
The last-named poet has expressed with exquisite
accuracy the characteristics of Locker's verse in these
well-known lines :

> *Apollo made, one April day,*
> *A new thing in the rhyming way ;*
> *Its turn was neat, its wit was clear,*
> *It wavered 'twixt a smile and tear ;*
> *Then Momus gave a touch satiric,*
> *And it became a "London Lyric."*

I forget how I had the good fortune to make Mr.
Locker's acquaintance, but I am inclined to think it
was through the kindness of Sir Edmund Gosse. He
must have been close on seventy when I first met him,
but he looked much younger, with his elegant im-
maculately clothed figure and his sprightly boyish air,
with something gay and birdlike in his alertly sympathetic manner. I have many of his charming letters,
filled with a courtly friendliness, and in one of these
he makes this interesting reference to John Godfrey
Saxe. Writing from Rowfant he says:

"When you come and see me here, I must show you
a curious book, written by John Godfrey Saxe, an
American poet, now dead. He calls it "Pensées"—and
only printed two copies, and this is one of the two. He
sent it me. The Poems are rather warmer than such

poems usually are. Something like Rossetti—I think
it will interest you, as it did me."

I never visited Locker at Rowfant, so never saw that
all-but-unique copy of Saxe, but a visit I paid him at
his house at Cromer lives like lavender in my memory
—and one incident of it in particular. My young wife
was with me. We were both pathetically young, almost
like two Babes in the Wood in the midst of the distinguished house party to which he had invited us. I
think our very youth and our *naïveté* must have touched
the spring of tenderness in him, never indeed difficult
to reach. However it was, he seemed to make us his
especial care, talking to us and watching over us with
quite a fatherly affection. And the incident I am particularly thinking of was this. When bedtime came on the
first night of our stay, he himself took us up to our
room in a little six-sided tower, and, looking around
to see that we were comfortable, he excused himself
a moment, and, after a short absence, returned with
two books under his arm, two small quartos fragrantly
bound in full morocco.

"I thought," he said, "that you might like to have
something with you to read, and I think I have brought
something appropriate for two such lovers."

Then, placing the books in our hands, he patted
us gently on the shoulders, nodded a smiling good-
night, and was gone. We turned eagerly to look at the
books, and what was our surprise and delight to find
that one of the volumes contained the love letters of
John Keats to Fanny Brawne, in the original manuscripts, and that the other contained some letters of
Shelley to Mary also in the original manuscripts!
Could any courtesy to two young people have been

more romantically conceived? And need one say what it meant to our young hearts? We were sleeping in the same room with the sacred love letters of Keats and Shelley, just as they had written them! Wonderful world! Wonderful, wonderful Mr. Locker!

Frederick Locker might be regarded as the elder brother of three poets, who at that time formed a very special triumvirate in the combined arts of poetry and criticism, poets who, like himself, cultivated the formal gardens of verse, poets of bric-à-brac and blue china, and those old French forms of ballade, rondeau, virelay, and the like, to which they brought a renewed vitality and gave a new vogue. I refer, of course, to Messrs. Lang, Dobson, and Gosse. In those days they were all mentioned together, as they will still go on being associated in their triune fame. Of the living it is not my purpose to speak in these random recollections, though I hope it will not be out of place, in passing, for me to acknowledge with gratitude the various kindnesses that I, in common with other young writers of my day, owe to Sir Edmund Gosse, and that eager sympathy with which he still continues to greet and encourage the younger generation, now more obstreperously than ever knocking at the door.

Austin Dobson I met only once or twice. Outside his intimates, he was socially in evidence but seldom, a quiet little domestic man who, when his day's work was ended, softly disappeared to his large family and his books. But he wrote me several friendly letters, in quaintly beautiful printed handwriting, for it was more like delicate printing than handwriting. His envelopes were miniature works of art, like one of his

own rondels; one could not think of destroying
them; rather one thought of taking them to some
exquisite picture-framer for an appropriate eighteenth-
century setting. They were usually sealed, too,
with a seal ring, a lovely intaglio of Diana seated
and stooping, with a tiny crescent moon over her
head.

Different indeed was the handwriting of Dobson's
poetical "neighbour of the near domain," Andrew
Lang. Broken, jagged, like a series of small rapid stabs
on the paper, disorderly and cynically careless of
appearances, it has the look of writing that had once
been good but had been ruined by an incessant and
often impatiently weary use of the pen, and indeed few
pens since writing was invented can have covered so
vast an acreage of paper or written upon such a variety
of themes. Outside his works of serious scholarship
and that serious poetry which was one deep disappointment of his life, there was always something scornful
and casual in his use of his pen. In one of his personal
lyrics he blames his Highland ancestors for having
condemned their child to a life of pen and ink. Could
he but have wielded the sword or smitten the lyre
instead! In spite of himself, however, it was a charmed
pen that Fate had put into his hand, a pen incapable
of being dull, whatever the subject, always wayward,
and whimsical, and magically light of touch, though
one seldom failed to detect the wistfulness of something lost or missed under the gay, mocking humour.
Perhaps it was only the constitutional melancholy of
the Celt, though, as I have hinted, the failure of "Helen
of Troy" to win acceptance was one definite dis-

illusionment, and the singer of that haunting love lyric—

> *Who wins his Love shall lose her,*
> *Who loses her shall gain . . .*

may well have had deeper causes of melancholy. But, though he wrote to Robert Louis Stevenson—

> *. . . man, I've maistly had my fill*
> *O' this world's din,*

there was never any weariness perceptible to the reader in that charmed pen. Only Theophile Gautier and Anatole France, to both of whom he bore resemblances, has ever made journalism such a debonair thing. One of the most finished and "superior" products of Oxford, wearing his panoply of learning as though it were a garment of iridescent gossamer, turning the driest subject to "favour and to prettiness," particularly the prettiness of an elfish, incalculable wit, no other such combination of poet, scholar, and journalist has been known in Fleet Street. One of the earliest of "colyumists"—but how different!—his "leaders" in the *Daily News* read like fairy-tales written by an erudite Puck. Of his offhand manner of writing those there are many anecdotes. Once he was staying at a country house for the week-end, and, remembering that his "leader" for the day was still to be written, he strolled into the billiard room, where some fellow guests were knocking about the balls, and, curling himself up on one of the settees, he began to scribble away, all the time keeping an interested eye on the game, till at last one of the players remarked that they feared they must be disturbing him. "Not in the least," he answered, "but are you sure I am not interfering with your game?"

On another occasion he was on the train, and his "leader" being once more on his mind, he looked around the compartment for something on which to rest his writing-pad. There was a farmer among the passengers wearing one of those old-fashioned square, flat-topped felt hats, a sort of rectangular "bowler." "The very thing!" Lang said to himself, and calmly requested the loan of it from its wearer, doubtless to the rustic's surprise. The request, however, was granted, and, placing the hat on his knee and the pad on the hat, Lang went to work, and in half an hour or so, with his usual rapidity, had produced his copy, on fairies, or golf, or the Greek Kalends, and returned his extemporized desk to its bewildered owner.

Above all things Lang hated to seem to take himself or his work seriously, as he abhorred all forms of "side" and "bosh," and, confirmatory of the slight anecdotes I have just related, he wrote in this way of a volume of his own verses:

> *They were scribbled in sketch-books or flybooks,*
> *In lectures, on lochs, by the seas ;*
> *And wherefore do people who buy books*
> *Go purchasing these?*

His dread of rhetorical gesture seems to have extended to the sound of his own name, which he always signed "A. Lang," as though "Andrew Lang" were too melodious and romantic. His practice in this respect was the precise opposite of Oscar Wilde's, of whom a story is told that an American friend once took him to a club and entered his name in the visitor's book as "O. Wilde."

" 'O. Wilde!' " said Oscar, "who is 'O. Wilde'? Nobody knows 'O. Wilde'—but 'Oscar Wilde' is a household word!"

Yet, of course, Lang was actually of romance all compact. He took up no study, however dry in appearance, that was not romantic at its core, and, after his dream of being a great poet had faded, his great desire was to write a romance after the manner of his hero Dumas, or his friend Robert Louis Stevenson, whose fame he had no small share in making. Here, alas! he was again doomed to disappointment, for "The Monk of Fife"—about which he wrote me several letters, almost pathetically concerned about its proper presentation to the public—fell as flat as his epic of "Helen of Troy." All his friends did their best for it in vain. In appearance Lang was decidedly romantic, as his portrait by Sir W. B. Richmond unmistakably shows, with his longish "brindled hair," and deep olive skin, and fine eyes, though the rather haughty languor of his expression and the amused scepticism around his mouth seemed to be deprecating the fact; and his later portraits look as though he were trying to be as prosaic as possible—as much as possible "A. Lang." He was, I think, a "too quick despairer" about his own poetry, and, charming as is such prose of his as "Letters to Dead Authors," "In the Wrong Paradise," and "Old Friends," I believe that it is his poetry that, after all, will keep his name alive, for his best ballades and lyrics have a fragrance and a *légèreté* nearer to the charm of his master Ronsard than anything else we have in England—not to forget his one great sonnet on "the surge and thunder of the Odyssey."

Among the men in the middle distance who were rapidly putting on immortality under our very eyes, perhaps the most important of all, as in certain directions the most influential, was another fine flower of Oxford culture—Walter Pater. Mr. George Moore has placed himself on record more than once to the effect that Pater's "Marius the Epicurean" is the most beautiful book in the English tongue. This was the opinion also of many young men in the '90s, and Pater's indeed is one of the fames of those days that has grown with time and is still growing. The individuality and solidity of his thought behind the sumptuous tapestry of his prose are more than ever realized, and what by many was once regarded as mere ornament is now seen to be an indispensable part of the construction. By his book on "The Renaissance" Pater was virtually the founder of the Aesthetic Movement, as he was the most potent influence on the school of young men of whom I shall later have to speak. In those days we were all going around quoting the famous description, or rather re-creation, of the Mona Lisa—"She is older than the rocks among which she sits," et cetera—and we were all exhorting each other "to burn always with this hard, gemlike flame," and to maintain that ecstasy which is the true success of life. Oscar Wilde popularized, and indeed somewhat vulgarized, as he perhaps to a degree misunderstood, and certainly dangerously applied, the gospel of beauty and "ecstasy" which Pater taught with hierarchical reserve and with subdued though intense passion and colour of words.

Of Pater's love of beautiful words Oscar Wilde told me a story which he may well have invented, but which, at all events, is good parody. In Pater's class at Oxford was a young man with the incredible name of "Sanctuary." On one occasion, Pater, before beginning his lecture, requested Mr. Sanctuary to remain behind at the end. Possibly Mr. Sanctuary apprehended trouble, for Pater was a proctor. However, when the lecture ended, the rest of the class having left the room, it was the Professor who was visibly embarrassed as he stood face to face with the student. After the embarrassment had lasted a few minutes, "You asked me to stay behind, sir, did you not?" said the young man.

"Oh, yes, Mr. Sanctuary," answered Pater, "I wanted to say to you—what a very beautiful name you have got!"

When I told Wilde one day that I was about to pay a visit to Oxford, and that I had hopes of seeing Pater, he indulged in another flight of parody, which, like all his vivid exaggerations of the kind, flashed a true portrait in caricature.

"So you are going to see Pater! That will be delightful. But I must tell you one thing about him, to save you from disappointment. You must not expect him to talk like his prose. Of course, no true artist ever does that. But, besides that, he never talks about anything that interests him. He will not breathe one golden word about the Renaissance. No! he will probably say something like this: 'So you wear cork soles in your shoes? Is that really true? And do you find them comfortable? . . . How extremely interesting!'"

When a few days later I met Pater at dinner, at the house of Mr. Daniels of the famous private press on which Mr. Robert Bridges' poems were first printed in now inaccessible editions, I realized the truth of Wilde's little fable. Not that I cared whether the author of "Marius" talked or not. As in the case of Swinburne, to be actually looking at him was marvel enough. If his conversation was unlike his writing, certainly no man's appearance was ever less like his books. Here indeed was no exquisite languishing "aesthete," such as his work might have misled one into fearing. On the contrary, he looked very much more like a Prussian officer, fully six feet tall, indeed, rather more I should say, strongly built, broad shouldered, soldierly erect, and, except for the gentleness in his eyes, rather too close together under a dome which almost entire baldness exaggerated, his large face was almost brutal with its blunt nose, jowlish chin, and a large heavy mouth over which hung an immense solid moustache of the kind known in England as a "mudguard." But this impression of brutality was immediately dissipated by the paradoxical gentleness and shy courtesy of his manner, so withdrawn and yet so sympathetic, almost maidenly, if one might use the word of so large and masculine a man. I cannot recall what he talked about, my impression is that he talked but little. I listened in hope that he really might mention cork soles, but if he did, his remarks have escaped me.

One little intimate impression I was to have of him, however, to carry back to town. As the time came for our party to break up. Pater asked me where I was staying, and, on hearing that my hostel was the Clarendon, he thrilled me by saying that, that being so, he would walk part way with me, as his home was at Brasenose near by. So we started, I having but one

thought, that I was walking side by side with the
Master whose writings had meant so much to my life.
Once again I was seeing Shelley plain, and with entire
content, for a great calm sympathy emanated from a
silence that seemed all made of gentle courtesy. His
silence was like that of some deep rich summer night—
and I entirely forgot those profane cork soles.

And then befell a quaint little incident. We were
walking down a sort of walled lane, and presently, in
an angle of it, we became aware of two young men
talking to two young women under a dimly burning
gas-lamp. As we came up to them, Pater suddenly
stopped, and adjusting his *pince-nez*, went up to the
young men and peered closely into one face and then
into the other, as though to fix them in his memory.
No one spoke a word, and we resumed our walk in
silence, till at length we came to the venerable gates of
Brasenose College.

"This is where I live, Le Gallienne," said Pater, "I
wish I could ask you in, but I'm afraid it is too late for
both of us." Then he paused a moment and resumed:

"Now there are two ways you can take to your hotel.
You can go this way," and he pointed with his hand,
"or you can go this way," pointing the way we had
come. He paused again, and then, with a little confiding
laugh, he added: "But I think you had better take this
way, for I'm afraid that if you were to take the other—
those naughty girls would get hold of you!"

With that sudden human touch we parted, and
naturally, I reflected as I went on, that I would rather
have heard Pater say that little human thing than talk
whole pages of the Renaissance. As I walked on, too,
the probable explanation of the little scene came to me.

Pater, as well as being the author of "Marius," was, as I have said, a proctor, and those two young men had trouble brewing for them on the morrow—yet trouble, I was sure, of no very serious nature. For the man who had said "those naughty girls" with so human an intonation could not, it was evident, be a very formidable proctor.

It was not, of course, only for his hedonistic doctrine that the younger school, of whom I shall next have to speak, valued Pater: it was perhaps even more because he was so fine an artist in prose, something like an English Flaubert; for at that time it was the art of prose, rather than that of verse, that occupied most of our minds. After Tennyson, Swinburne, and Bridges, it seemed as though the art of verse could go no further. Besides, prose was a more plastic medium, lending itself more sensitively to the impress of individual temperament; perhaps the more difficult for that. At all events, it seemed, so to say, to have more future than verse; less had been done with it; and many young pundits declared it the great art of the two. What solemn talks I have heard on the subject in the elaborate periods of Oscar Wilde and in the vivacious, whimsical harangues of Henry Harland!

Of this great art Pater was the acknowledged Master, but there was another who had devoted himself, in a peculiarly strenuous apprenticeship, to the same art, whose essays we were also reading with great respect and admiration—Robert Louis Stevenson, whose flight to Samoa had added the last crowning touch of canonizing romance to that "legend" of him which was even then complete. Unlike Pater, who kept the secrets of his art to himself, Stevenson, with perhaps too much of that autobiographic expansiveness which has since become so wearily usual and tasteless, had exhibited his writing desk in public, and discussed his own methods, his "sedulous ape" self-training, in front of the literary footlights. To be thus taken into his confidence was charming, but I think it was unwise for his fame, as it kept us on the look-out for artificiality in his work, and made us inclined to forget that, after all, it was natural for him to write, and that what is good in him came from deep springs which neither he nor any other critic can trace very far. By his own insistence on the acquired craftsmanship of his art he ran the risk of belittling the genius without which all his sedulous aping had been in vain.

I never knew that gay beloved figure, though I once came near to him in this letter that one morning fell out of the sky to me, headed "Vailima, Samoa," and made me walk on air for many days.

VAILIMA, SAMOA,
December 28th, 1893.

DEAR MR. LE GALLIENNE,

I have received some time ago, through our friend Miss Taylor, a book of yours. But that was by no means my first introduction to your name. The same book had stood already on my shelves; I had read articles of yours in the *Academy*; and by a piece of constructive criticism (which I trust was sound) had arrived at the conclusion that you were a Log-roller. Since then I have seen your beautiful verses to your wife. You are to conceive me, then, as only too ready to make the acquaintance of a man who loved good literature and could make it. I had to thank you, besides, for a triumphant exposure of a paradox of my own: the literary-prostitute disappeared from view at a phrase of yours—"the essence is not in the pleasure but the sale." True: you are right, I was wrong; the author is not the whore, but the libertine; and yet I shall let the passage stand. It is an error, but it illustrated the truth for which I was contending, that literature—painting—all art, are no other than pleasures, which we turn into trades.

And more than all this, I had and I have to thank you for the intimate loyalty you have shown to myself; for the eager welcome you give to what is good—for the courtly tenderness with which you touch on my defects. I begin to grow old; I have given my top note, I fancy;—and I have written too many books. The world begins to be weary of the old booth; and if not weary, familiar with the familiarity that breeds contempt. I do not know that I am sensitive to criticism, if it be hostile; I am sensitive indeed, when it is friendly; and when I read such criticism as yours, I am emboldened to go on and praise God.

You are still young, and you may live to do much. The little artificial popularity of style in England tends, I think, to die out; the British pig returns to his true love, the love of the style-less, of the shapeless, of the slapdash and the disorderly. Rudyard Kipling, with all his genius, his Morrowbie-Jukess, and At-the-end-of-the-Passages, is a move in that direction, and it is the wrong one. There is trouble coming, I think; and you may have to hold the fort for us in evil days.

Lastly, let me apologize for the crucifixion that I am inflicting on you (*bien à contre coeur*) by my bad writing. I was once the best of writers; landladies, puzzled as to my "trade," used to have their honest bosoms set at rest by a sight of a page of manuscript.—"Ah," they would say, "no wonder they pay you for that";— and when I sent it in to the printers, it was given to the boys! I was about thirty-nine, I think, when I had a turn of scrivener's palsy; my hand got worse; and for the first time, I received clean proofs. But it has gone beyond that now, I know I am like my old friend James Payn, a terror to correspondents; and you will not believe the care with which this has been written.

Believe me to be, very sincerely yours,

ROBERT LOUIS STEVENSON.

I came near to Stevenson, too, in the person of his lifelong friend and crony, the companion of his early escapades in Edinburgh, Charles Baxter. My encounter with Baxter was of such a nature that I had no difficulty in understanding that historic friendship, and the deep earth-roots of it, for of all the boon companions I have met or read of Charles Baxter was the amazing prince. He was a preposterously vital and imaginative talker, ample of frame, with a voice like a colonel of cavalry, and what a swashbuckler he would have made in the heroic days his friend loved to write of! With what an air of braggadocio he would have gone clanking into a tavern, with his long sword, and high boots, and feathered hat! It was in an old London tavern that our acquaintance first began, early one afternoon; night fell and we were still there, and when the morning star began to fade and the dawn to press her white face at the window, there were we still, to breakfast over Scotch kippers and sirloin steaks, washed down with draughts Elizabethan. Yes! it was a night at the

Mermaid—but, alas! no one can spend such a night with the redoubtable Charles any more; for, if he had any enemies, he is now lustily engaged in drinking wine out of their skulls in some thunderously mirthful Valhalla.

Nearer still I came to "Tusitala" later on in New York, where I had the happiness of several meetings with Mrs. Stevenson, the "Fanny" for whom he had crossed the seas steerage (or rather, I think, "second cabin"), crossed the continent of America in an emigrant train, and almost starved to death in San Francisco.

To know Mrs. Stevenson, with her splendid leonine head, her great hypnotic eyes, and her overwhelming magnetism was easily to understand her lover's devotion. In the talks I had with her she told me many vivid things about her husband, and particularly impressive was the account she gave me of his sudden dying, there on the steps of his Vailima verandah, just as he was gaily making a salad and discoursing on a special wine for their dinner that night, a dinner to be as festive as possible, to drive away the black clouds of ill omen that had been oppressing her for several days with an unbearable sense of coming doom—for, as will appear from an anecdote I shall presently tell, Mrs. Stevenson was very evidently a "psychic."

Talking of wine, she told me an amusing story of Stevenson in their early days in France. Like many sensitive, gentle-mannered men, Stevenson was subject to sudden storms of rage, particularly when aroused by what he deemed an injustice to others or by an insolence to himself. They were all peaceably dining one evening in some French restaurant, I forget

THE ROMANTIC '90S

where—perhaps at Barbizon—when, tasting the wine
which had been set before them—and of wine he was
something of a connoisseur—Stevenson declared that
it was "corked" and ordered the proprietor to bring
another bottle. The offending bottle was removed with
many apologies, and another bottle, lying aslant in its
wicker basket, deferentially brought. When Stevenson
presently made trial of that, his ire suddenly sprang up
like flame, for not only was the new bottle also "corked," but he was convinced that a trick had been played
upon him, and that the identical wine he had rejected
had merely been taken out of the room and brought
back again. Nothing would persuade him otherwise,
and rising from the table, white with silent rage, he
seized the bottle by the neck, and whirling it round his
head, careless that its contents were pouring down his
coat sleeve, he strode majestically through the room,
till he came close up to one of the walls, against which
he dashed it to pieces in a very satisfying fury. Having
thus relieved himself by this startling mode of expression, he seated himself, once more calm, at the table,
and the dinner resumed its peaceful laughing course.

The other anecdote to which I referred brings
Charles Baxter into the story in a sufficiently mysterious
and characteristically amusing manner. It was the
winter up at Saranac, where Stevenson had been
recommended for the benefit of his lungs, and where
he wrote "The Silverado Squatters." A very bright
sunlit forenoon, with the reflected light from the snow
dazzling in at all the windows. Mrs. Stevenson was
alone reading in one of the rooms, when suddenly she
was surprised by seeing Charles Baxter enter, over-
coated as for a journey and evidently in a fury of rage.

She gazed at him intense and natural astonishment, for she knew that he could not be in America at that moment, knew indeed that he was far off in England. Then, as she gazed at the irate figure, it gradually disappeared, fading out on the snow-lit air. Thereupon she ran out of the room, seeking her husband.

"I have just seen Charles," she said, "and he seemed in a frightful rage about something."

Stevenson, who was aware of his wife's "psychic" peculiarities, took it naturally, and said, "All right, Fanny—let's see what time it is," and, looking at his watch, he made careful note of the hour and minute. Days and weeks passed, and at last came the explanation. It appears that on that morning Baxter was travelling on the London and South Western Railway, in England. Before boarding the train, he bought at the railway bookstall a copy of "The Wrong Box," written by Stevenson and his stepson, Mr. Lloyd Osbourne. It had only just been published, and he was naturally curious about it. It is an amusing book, and one can imagine his enjoying it for awhile, till suddenly, so the story went, he came upon a character in it which he conceived to be an offensive caricature of himself. Enraged, he read on, till he could stand it no longer, and, rising from his seat, he hurled the book out of the window, far across the flying country-side. It was at that precise moment that he appeared to Mrs. Stevenson in her Saranac sitting-room.

Here surely is a story that deserves a place in Professor Gurney's book of "Phantasms of the Living." I tell it as nearly as I can recall it as Mrs. Stevenson told it to me.

III

THE death of Tennyson in 1892 was perhaps the most impressive event of my first years in London. It seemed even more than the death of a great poet, and it touched the imagination as giving dramatic emphasis to the passing of the old Victorian order of which, more than any other, he had been the spiritual and intellectual spokesman, one might even say prophet, the inspired, magnificent "*vates*." It had been easy while he lived to tell amusing stories about his gruffness and his vanity, and to set against the picture of him evoked by Meredith, I must be allowed to parenthesize this more companionable and all-round portrait of him at the age of thirty-three made by that master of pen-portraiture Thomas Carlyle:

"One of the finest-looking men in the world. A great shock of rough, dusky, dark hair; bright, laughing hazel eyes; massive aquiline face, most massive yet most delicate; of sallow brown complexion, almost Indian-looking, clothes cynically loose, free-and-easy, smokes infinite tobacco. His voice is musical, metallic, fit for loud laughter and piercing wail, and all that may lie between; speech and speculation free and plenteous; I do not meet in these late decades such company over a pipe." And Carlyle, we may remember, was not easily pleased.

While a great man lives it is human to make fun over his foibles, and long before Tennyson's death the revolt against his poetic supremacy had set in, and the younger men had already begun to sneer at his art, and quote Swinburne's gibe against the "Idylls of the King," which, he said, would have been more appropriately entitled "Mort d'Albert, or Idylls of the Prince Consort." Nevertheless, the general feeling among men of letters, as with "the man in the street," was that expressed by Andrew Lang—"The Master's yonder in the Isle"—the isle, of course, being the Isle of Wight. While he lived, we somehow felt more secure, secure for the position of poetry in a world which needed such a figure to maintain its august estate. This Tennyson did as few poets have ever done. He looked the great poet, his life had been lived consistently as a great poet, and his place in the English world of the day was exalted, enthroned, with even a touch of sacredness, such as that which attaches to a great cardinal. The image is worn enough, but his passing was like the fall of a great oak in a forest of lesser trees. As it crashes down, the landscape seems to grow suddenly empty, devoid of meaning, filled with the naked light of common day.

When Byron died, it had seemed to Tennyson that poetry had fled from the earth, and Tennyson's own death made a like gap in a world of smaller men and lesser voices. No one who was present at his funeral in Westminster Abbey will ever forget its solemn grandeur, its symbolic impressiveness. For several days England had seemed to be holding its breath at his bedside, and, when the end came, it read with something like awe the dramatic story of his last hours— how he had asked to have the blinds up, for, he said, "I want to see the sky and the light"; how he had said to the doctor, "What a shadow this life is, and how men cling to what is after all but a small part of the great world's life"; and again, how he had whispered to the doctor the question "Death?" and, when the doctor bowed his head, he had answered "That's well." A telegram of inquiry from Queen Victoria, which he had been able to answer, was also a detail not the least impressive to the popular imagination. Here was greatness all could understand! And the final moon-lit scene. Tennyson had been the poet magnificently in his life, but what poet ever died a poet's death with such picturesque and touching majesty? Had his friend Henry Irving arranged his deathbed it could not have been a finer piece of dramatic art. When death was near he had asked for his folio Shakespeare, and as the moonlight flooded with its strange radiance his kingly figure and the great page he had loved so well, his hand rested peacefully among the leaves of that play of "Cymbeline" which contains the most heart-breaking of all threnodies:

> *Fear no more the heat o' the sun*
> *Nor the furious winter's rages;*
> *Thou thy earthly task hast done,*
> *Home art gone and ta'en thy wages. . . .*

And there, when death came, his hand lay still, at rest on the moonlit page.

His burial in the Abbey was a ceremony of an indescribable thrilling solemnity. One seemed to be aware of all London, standing hushed and bare-headed outside the old walls, and within were gathered to do him honour all the great and distinguished and beautiful men and women of his land. Among them all particularly stands out for me the wild-rose face of

Ellen Terry. Nobles and men of genius bore the pall of the vast laurelled coffin, as it advanced beneath the soaring arches of exquisitely fretted stone to its place of rest near Chaucer in the corner dedicated to the great poets of England, while, sung as it seemed by disembodied voices, the strains of his own "Crossing the Bar" filled the memoried twilight of painted windows and dim chapels, crowded with the tombs of the illustrious dead and the scutcheons of kings and princes; and suddenly a voice of piercing ethereality was heard singing the strangely haunted words of that poem "The Silent Voices," which he had written a few days before his death:

> *When the dumb Hour, clothed in black,*
> *Brings the Dreams about my bed,*
> *Call me not so often back,*
> *Silent Voices of the dead,*
> *Towards the lowland ways behind me,*
> *And the sunlight that is gone!*
> *Call me rather, silent Voices,*
> *Forward to the starry track*
> *Glimmering up the heights beyond me*
> *On, and always on!*

Amid all the solemnity there was a curious exalted joyousness, as of a celestial springtide uplifting the heart, that sad October day, a strange gladness breaking through the sorrow of the music. It was less like an ending of mortal greatness than a triumphal entry into immortality. "Carry the last great bard to his last bed," William Watson had written in his noble elegy, yet it seemed not funeral but divine honours that a great nation was here paying to its great poet. The laurels on his coffin seemed less the laurels of the dead than the laurels of the victor, and one felt that the farewell we were making was not to a long, illustrious life descending into everlasting sleep but to a lofty spirit ascending to his place. That which had drawn from out the boundless deep was but turning again home.

Within two years another great poet of a later generation, William Morris, was to be carried to his rest, also in an appropriately dramatic, though simple and idyllic, manner. I never knew Morris, but I saw him once at an afternoon meeting, held for the discussion of some artistic scheme, I forget what, in the London house of the Duke of Westminster. Oscar Wilde took me there, and I remember how, as we walked through the spacious and lofty rooms, on the walls of which hung gigantic paintings by some master I cannot recall extending from ceiling to floor, Wilde made one of his magnificent gestures and said to me, "Ah! Richard, this is how a gentleman should live!" Wilde was to be among the speakers, who were already seated on a raised platform, the Duke himself and several distinguished writers amongst them. The proceedings were well under way, when a thick-set, wide-shouldered, burly figure, somehow recalling to me Cedric, the Saxon thane, in "Ivanhoe," with a massive rugged head and broad ruddy open face, jovial and yet suggestive of nervous irascibilty, blundered in, like a huge bumble-bee into a quiet room on a summer afternoon, and making a hurried, rather embarrassed attempt to mount the platform stumbled and almost fell with an uncouth clatter, an incident which provoked a titter of irreverent laughter in the discreet audience. It was William Morris.

Dressed in his shirt of socialist blue, with a flowing tie, and in clothes of rough blue serge, he looked more like a sea captain than a poet, a comparison he would have welcomed. Certainly no one could have looked less like "the idle singer of an empty day," and one was surprised to find so robust an envelope for the spirit whose poetry was of so dreamy a sensuousness and of so honeyed a melancholy. It was not Morris the poet who stood before us and presently addressed us, but Morris the Master Craftsman, the creator of Morris chairs, wall-papers, and tapestries, and the Master Printer of the Kelmscott Press, whose missal-like editions we were all then eagerly collecting.

Only a short while after, an ox-cart, wreathed with vines and country garlands, moved slowly towards Kelmscott churchyard, followed "by the workmen whom he had inspired, the members of the Socialist League which he had supported, the students of the art guild he had founded, and the villagers who had learnt to love him." It was more like a rural festival than a funeral, resembling one of the many idyllic pro- cessionals in his own poems, and it was a leave-taking conceived according to his own attitude towards death, as a joyous rather than a sorrowful adventure.

A year or two after, wandering haphazard about England on a bicycle, I came with a thrill of surprise upon a finger-post which said "To Kelmscott," and soon I was making my way to the little churchyard. It is a sad stone village, is Kelmscott—sad with some- thing of the sadness of the stone villages of the Cots- wolds. The hard life of the earth seems to have made grim the wintry faces of the buildings, as it makes grim the faces of old farm hands that have feared God for eighty years, yet with just that sweetness which comes of being worn and worn, like old silver. It is a place of many trees, which crowd shelteringly close around the tiny church, with its one great grave. Grave so great, yet almost hidden away beneath the boundary hedge of the churchyard—a careless, mouldering place, where no official sexton disturbs the dead with nicely ordered gravel and packets of forget-me-not, but where the moss creeps stealthily in the night of forgetfulness and the weeds fearlessly thicken. Just a sarcophagus of plain stone with a touch of simple beauty in its shape and: "William Morris, 1834-1896." As I stood there I found myself saying to myself some words from one of those beautiful prose romances by Morris which are perhaps more truly himself than his poetry:

. . . and Ralph said: "How is it with thee, beloved?"
"O well, indeed," she said.
Quoth he: "And how tasteth to thee the water of the Well?"
Slowly she spake and sleepily: "It tasteth good, and as if thy love were blended in it."

And then I turned away from "The Well at the World's End," and came to the end of the lane—a cul-de-sac of great trees, with the young Thames just below, lying like a nymph among the reeds, and before long found myself before the grey gables of Kelmscott House, a lovely old Jacobean manor full of ancient peace.

Morris, for all his vast output of various work, was but sixty-two when he died, and his beautiful wife was still alive. The temptation to look upon the face of

Jane Burden, whose strange loveliness dreams out at us from the paintings of Rossetti, the very Muse of the pre-Raphaelite brotherhood, was too great to be resisted, and presently I was seated with her, tall and stately and lovelier perhaps for a touch of the years on her splendid hair, taking tea at the foot of the old sunny orchard, where, I said to myself, Rossetti too had once sat and painted her on just such an afternoon. I remember that we had some particularly good quince jam with our tea, and, on remarking upon its goodness, "I made it myself," said the Blessed Damozel, "and, as you like it so much, you shall have a jar to take with you." A jar of quince jam made by the beautiful lady whom Morris had loved and Rossetti had painted! It was like receiving it at the hands of Helen of Troy. But before I took it away with me, Mrs. Morris led me into the house, into his study, with his books as he had left them, the superb Kelmscott Chaucer, which he and Burne-Jones had made together, lying open on the table, and tapestries woven by himself hanging on the walls. It was a dream-like afternoon, and, as I departed with my quince jam, it seemed to me that it must indeed have come to me in a dream. I cannot recall now what became of it. Perhaps it vanished back into dreamland, for it cannot be conceived that it was eaten in commonplace fashion, like other earthly jams.

Tennyson and Morris had thus gone, but, as we have seen, two of the famous pre-Raphaelite brotherhood still vigorously survived, Swinburne and Meredith, and were to live on well into the present century, both dying in the same year, 1909. One other major Victorian poet survived with them, Coventry Patmore, whose celebration of domestic love in "The Angel in

the House," in which the Wife figures somewhat unusually as the Muse, had won great popularity, but
whose finest poetry is to be found in "The Unknown
Eros." I once met Patmore, who belongs to the small
but rare band of Catholic poets, in the charming home
circle of Mr. and Mrs. Wilfrid Meynell. He was a tall,
distinguished man, hidalgo-like in his rather haughty
reserve. I do not recall his talk, but he once wrote me a
letter on a volume of my youthful verses, in which he
gave me a piece of advice I have always kept by me,
and, I hope, have since profited by. "Like many young
poets," he said, "you live too much on the capital,
rather than on the interest, of passion." He meant, of
course, that my verse made too much use of the raw
material of immediate personal experience, instead of
allowing it to mature and refine itself in the mind towards a genuine poetical distillation. It is a piece of
advice which I hand on to the present generation of
poets, whose need of it is great, and to whom Mr.
Brownell has recently been giving a like counsel when
he writes of "depth of feeling, purified of transitory
intensities."

Here is a fitting place for me to pay a tribute of
memory to that home circle of the Meynells to which
I have just referred. Mrs. Alice Meynell, known for
that one sonnet of "Renouncement" which belongs
with the great sonnets of love and esteemed, too, for
her distinguished essays so deeply meditated and
wrought with so finely selective an economy of
"unique" words, was then, as for long after, a veritable
Egeria in the London literary world, the centre of a
salon that recalled the salons of pre-Revolutionary
France. Meredith could not literally sit at her feet, for

his illness chained him to Box Hill, but in spirit he was there, devotedly attentive, during the closing years of his life, as his letters and later poems bear witness. But never surely was a lady who carried her learning and wore the flower of her gentle humane sanctity with such quiet grace, with so gentle and understanding a smile. The touch of exquisite asceticism about her seemed but to accent the sensitive sympathy of her manner, the manner of one quite humanly and simply in this world, with all its varied interests, and yet not of it. There was the charm of a beautiful abbess about her, with the added *esprit* of intellectual sophistication. However quietly she sat in her drawing-room of an evening with her family and friends about her, her presence radiated a peculiarly lovely serenity, like a twilight gay with stars. But there was nothing austere or withdrawn about her. In that very lively household of young people, girls and boys since grown up to write very individual books for themselves, she was one with the general fun, which under the direction of her buoyant, genial husband—appropriately the editor of a magazine called *Merry England*, and still, I am glad to think, one of the best *raconteurs* in London—used often to wax fast and furious and made dinner there a particularly exhilarating occasion. I give thanks here for the many joyous hours I have spent at that laughing board, and I have no other such picture of a full and harmonious home life to set by its side.

I like to recall that I was free of that household because of our common bond of admiration for the poetry of Francis Thompson. It had been my fortunate opportunity, as I have hinted in regard to Swinburne, to read that poetry in manuscript and accept it for publication by Mr. John Lane. It was, too, a feather in my critical cap with the Meynells that I wrote the first review of Thompson that was published, and had it out, in the *Daily Chronicle*, three days before any other review appeared. To act in the dual capacity of publisher's reader and reviewer had, I suppose, a reprehensible suspicion of "log-rolling" about it—a suspicion, I fear, which I often incurred in those days—but I'm afraid I am still blind to the offence of honestly praising in public what I had honestly accepted in private.

I saw Francis Thompson one evening there, but I cannot say that he made a great impression upon me. He seemed a rather ineffective personality, sitting silent and shrunken within himself, but it was probably his shy reserve that gave me that impression, and among his familiars, I am told, he was a different being. Of course, the Meynells had been his "discoverers" before myself or anyone else, and the story of Mr. Meynell's discovery of him is one of the most dramatic stories of the time. It has been told at length and delightfully by Mr. Everard Meynell in his "Life" of the poet. But in brief it was this. To the office of *Merry England* came one day the manuscript of an essay on "Paganism Old and New," and some poems. They were accompanied by a letter from the author in which he apologized for "the soiled state of the manuscript," and gave the Charing Cross Post Office as his address. The manuscripts were pigeon-holed for six months, and Mr. Meynell, on unearthing them, was so impressed that he wrote at once to Thompson, to receive his letter back some days later from the Dead Letter Office. He thereupon printed the "Passion of Mary," and soon after received a letter from Thompson, whom he invited to call at the office, but, having no further word from him, he set out to track him down. At last he got news of him at a chemist's shop in Drury Lane, where the poet was in the habit of buying opium, and where Mr. Meynell left him another invitation to call at the office. Many days afterwards "Mr. Thompson" was announced, a frightened tatterdemalion figure, "more ragged and unkempt than the average beggar, with no shirt beneath his coat and bare feet in broken shoes." As a medical student in Manchester, incipient tuberculosis and the reading of De Quincey had tempted him to the alleviation of opium, and thereafter for three years he had led a life of destitution, a life of the gutter and park benches, low lodging houses and refuges, the companion of tramps and beggars, thieves and even murderers, an outcast among outcasts. It was from this underworld that he had suddenly emerged, so dismaying an apparition, that day in Mr. Meynell's office, and it was from this life, with infinite tact and loving-kindness, that Mr. and Mrs. Meynell at last rescued him and persuaded his proud spirit to make his home with them. Not the least attractive part of the story is the devotion with which he repaid their goodness, a devotion of which his lovely "Sister-Songs," written for Mr. and Mrs. Meynell's two little daughters, is an enduring monument.

Mrs. Meynell's circle was, of course, but one of the many influential groups, or *cénacles*, of that energetic seminal period, each one with its chosen idolized prophet, and all, in one way or another, independently contributing to the creation of a new age. *Fin de siècle* was the label, with something of a stigma, which was used to cover them all, but, as one looks back, it is plain that here was not so much the ending of a century as the beginning of a new one. Those last ten years of the nineteenth century properly belong to the twentieth century, and, far from being "decadent," except in certain limited manifestations, they were years of an immense and multifarious renaissance. All our present conditions, socially and artistically, our vaunted new "freedoms" of every kind—including "free verse"—not only began then, but found a more vital and authoritative expression than they have found since because of the larger, more significant personalities engaged in bringing them about. As often happens, the pioneers were bigger men and women than those who have since entered into the new world they opened up, and who, in many cases, it may be thought, have pushed their conclusions to a *reductio ad absurdum*. Such achievements as the twentieth century can boast are merely extensions of what the men and women of the '90s began, and perhaps to-day we have less sowing, or even reaping, than running to seed. However that be, there is nothing that seems "new" just now to anyone familiar with the work done in those ten years nor have we made any discoveries that were not then already discovered, fought for, and written for.

Generally speaking, all our present-day developments amount to little more than pale or exaggerated copying of the '90s. The amount of creative revolutionary energy packed into that amazing decade is almost bewildering in its variety. So much was going on at once, in so many directions, with so passionate a fervour. A three-ringed circus gives but a small idea of the different whirling activities. In fact, London was more like a ten-ringed circus, with vividly original performers claiming one's distracted attention in every ring. Or perhaps one might better compare it to a series of booths at a fair, each with its vociferous "barker" inviting us in to the only show on earth. Outside one of them, called the *Scots*, and afterwards the *National Observer*, W. E. Henley, truculently announcing himself as the captain of his soul, was beating the big drum of Imperialism, supported by a band of brilliant young literary swordsmen, swearing by Mr. Rudyard Kipling, Mr. H. G. Wells, and Stevenson, and threatening to eat alive most other writers whatsoever.

Another mystic-looking booth, flying a green flag with an Irish harp figured upon it, was presided over by a cabalistical young poet, Mr. W. B. Yeats, musically talking of Rosicrucianism, fairies, Celtic folklore, and an Irish theatre, and backed by Irish scholars proclaiming the revival of the Gaelic tongue as the certain cure-all for Ireland's wrongs. Another Irishman, a witty, clowning fellow with a deadly method in his madness, was advertising Fabian socialism as a nostrum for all our national ills and discoursing on Wagner and the "Quintessence of Ibsenism" by the way; and sometimes as a vivacious interlude, stepping down to put on the gloves with some dissentient member of the audience, after the manner of his professional friend "Cashel Byron."

Then there were Socialist clergymen, preaching High Church Anglicanism, and pre-Raphaelite art for the slums of Whitechapel. Dudley Hardy was making dashing posters outside another booth—for it was the heyday of the poster—and at the door of another, Mr. Whistler, with a white forelock like a feather for his *panache*, was declaiming the paradoxes of his "Ten o'Clock" to a select and ecstatic gathering of devotees. All these and many other spirited performers met with mingled enthusiasm and jeers from the gaping crowds, hardly knowing what to make of some of them; but there is scarcely one of them whom Time has not justified, and whose wildest dreams have not become the realities of the twentieth century.

Mr. Kipling has taken Tennyson's place as the national bard and seer; Ireland is free and telegrams are accepted in Gaelic; the Abbey Theatre is a national Irish institution, and Mr. Yeats has won the Nobel prize. It is perhaps too bad to call Mr. Shaw a classic and to say that he has shocked the world so successfully that he can shock it no more, but such are among the recent surprises of Time's whirligig. The Fabian Society and William Morris's Hammersmith socialism have grown into a Labour Party, and political "dreamers" such as Sidney Webb and Sidney Oliver have become Cabinet Ministers, and even knights as well.

One important phase of the time should not be forgotten, that movement for the "New Theatre" which has since flourished like a green bay tree and brought forth so numerous a progeny of "little theatres," and new schools of drama, and theatric art generally. The honour of this belongs to J. T. Grein, whose "Independent Theatre," founded in 1892, was the father of them all. Appropriately enough, the first play, or one of the first, to be produced by Mr. Grein was "Widowers' Houses," by Mr. Shaw. The leading part, "Lickcheese," in this play was taken by James Welch, a young actor who afterwards became a popular comedian in such farcical comedies as "When

Knights were Bold," but whose real genius lay in such parts of tragi-comedy as Robson used to play, and with Robson Welch was often compared. Welch was well known for his wit in the '90s, and his early death was a great loss to the stage. Of all the early Shaw enthusiasts he was the most persistent, and, long before Mr. Shaw came into his own, Welch tried manfully to win him a London public. It is hard to realize nowadays, when Mr. Shaw is a millionaire prince of the theatre, what a struggle it was to get him on the stage. His earlier productions were merely brilliant flashes in the pan, and the longest run he had, before Mr. Arnold Daly started his vogue in New York with "Candida," was a fortnight of "Arms and the Man" at the Avenue Theatre. I remember well its eventful first night. The house was packed with Shaw enthusiasts, who, at the close of the play, summoned Mr. Shaw before the curtain, and clamouring for a speech, gave him the opportunity of making one of his readiest *mots*. Clad in his famous pepper-and-salt Jaeger clothes, his very beard seeming "Jaeger"—"Oh, Shaw!" said Oscar Wilde, "that's the man who smokes the Jaeger cigarettes!"— Mr. Shaw stood a moment, waiting for the applause to subside, when from the gallery came one decided "boo" of dissent. Looking up at the booer, with his irresistible Irish smile, he began his speech with "Personally, I agree with my friend in the gallery—but what can we two do against an audience of such a different opinion!" Mr. Shaw had not been heckled at the end of oratorical cart-tails in Hyde Park for nothing.

There is an anecdote told of him and James Welch which illustrates his appreciation of wit in other men. Welch was anxious to produce "You Never Can Tell," and went down into the country to see Mr. Shaw and talk terms. As usual, Mr. Shaw put a particularly lofty price on himself, a price Welch couldn't afford, and he left disappointed. Back in London, however, the notion came to him to try Shaw with a telegram running, "Why not give me the play for nothing?" The absurdity of the suggestion seems to have tickled Mr. Shaw so much that he immediately wired back a reply in the affimative.

While I am talking of Mr. Shaw, I may perhaps so far depart from my rule of not gossiping about contemporaries in these vagrom recollections as to recall a charming occasion which I am sure Mr. Shaw will not mind my telling about. At the time we were neighbours at Hindhead, near Haslemere, in Surrey, where Grant Allen and Sir Conan Doyle also had their country homes. The tiny schoolhouse there was presided over by an accomplished lady, herself with a pretty wit, who was anxious to interest her children in the wild life of the surrounding country-side, and had, therefore, got up a juvenile natural history club, which she asked Mr. Shaw to address. Happening to meet Mr. Shaw during the afternoon, he invited me to go with him to the meeting, to give him my moral support, he said; for he pretended, incredible as it may sound, to be nervous, as, in fact, I am inclined to think he really was. Inured to all manner of audiences, hostile, indifferent, and devoted, he had never yet talked to boys and girls. What on earth was he to say to them? As we entered the little schoolroom he noticed on the wall one of those game-preservation notices, giving particulars of the "close" periods, during which no one might hunt certain birds and beasts, under heavy penalties. Mr. Shaw detached the notice from the wall, and, when the school mistress had duly introduced him to his quite infantile audience, he rose with it in his hands. He began by reading certain passages. Then, turning to the children, he remarked that probably they had got the idea from what he had read that the grown-up people made such laws because of their great love for animals, because they couldn't bear the thought of their being killed. Nothing of the sort, my dear children, proceeded the archrebel against social hypocrisies, nothing of the sort! Their real meaning was, he continued, that they wanted you and me—and he adopted a confidential tone, as, so to say, a fellow youngster with themselves—to leave the birds, and rabbits, and other wild things alone, so that when the shooting season commenced there would be all the more of them—for the grown-ups themselves to shoot! It was not because they loved animals—but because they liked shooting them! This was the gist of his theme, which was received by the youngsters with peals of laughter, becoming still more uproarious as he went on to say that this was a sample of all the laws made by grown-ups for the young, and when from this he proceeded to deduce that the first duty of a child was to disobey its parents, and grown-ups generally, there was no controlling the delight of those happy little boys and girls. Never, of course, had they heard such talk before. Here was a friend of their young hearts indeed! When Shaw ended there was a small riot in that schoolroom, and the mistress held up her hands in amused dismay.

But, as I said, she was witty herself, and she rose to the occasion in a spirited reply. It was all very well, she said, for Mr. Shaw to talk like that to her young charges, but he had to deal with them for that night only, while she had them the whole year round, and it would take weeks for her to bring them back to law and order once more. So Mr. Shaw sowed the good seed of rebellion, in season and out, and I am sure he never won an audience so completely as he won those Hindhead children. I am sure, too, that he must count that little address on the game laws among the most flattering triumphs of his audacious tongue.

That "Celtic Movement," which was one of the marked and most far-reaching of the many movements of the '90s, was by no means entirely in the hands of Irishmen. Indeed, its first inception must be credited to Matthew Arnold's lectures "On the Study of Celtic Literature" as far back as 1867, though it was not till twenty years later that those lectures began to bear appreciable fruit. By then "Celticism" was very much in the air, and Grant Allen, who was one of the most barometric minds of the time, and one of the most vigorous and persuasive of all trumpeters of "advance" in every form, began one of his *Fortnightly Reviews* review articles, entitled "Celtic," with the characteristically dashing challenge, he being of Irish blood himself: "We Celts henceforth will rule the roost in Britain." That he was a true prophet who will gainsay?

Among those who after Mr. Yeats, contributed most to the Celtic triumph—or shall we say obsession?—was the Scotsman, William Sharp, better known to fame as "Fiona Macleod." The story of Sharp's "dual personality" was one of the most picturesque sensations of the '90s, as it was one of the cleverest hoaxes—if it was a hoax—in literary history. When I reached London, Sharp was already known as the biographer of Rossetti, the editor of an excellent anthology of sonnets, a popularizer of poetry, as editor of the famous "Canterbury" series, model of many such to follow, something of a poet himself, and generally an all-round *littérateur* of parts. He had read much and done a great deal of romantic travelling. But it was his personality that mattered most. He was probably the handsomest man in London, a large flamboyant "sun-god" sort of a creature, with splendid, vital, curling gold hair and a pointed golden beard, the bluest of Northern eyes, and the complexion of a girl. Laughing energy radiated from his robust frame, and he was all exuberance, enthusiasm, and infectious happiness, a veritable young Dionysus. If only he had been as good a poet as he was good-looking! But it would have been hard for writing to live up to such a victorious appearance, and, whenever his writing fell short, as for all its excellent critical qualities it sometimes did, it seemed to matter little, for he himself was success enough. No one could know him without falling under the spell of his generous magnetic nature, and I was proud to count him among my dearest friends. I don't mean to imply that his poetry was bad, but it disappointed one from so inadequately expressing himself —William Sharp. One felt that there was a poet behind it, a poet struggling to embody fine intuitions and imaginings, with insufficient mastery of the poetic art. The fact was that he had not yet found his medium, for all his experimenting with *vers librè*, of which, in *Sospiri di Roma*, he was one of the earliest pioneers. His best things were to be found in a volume of "Romantic Ballads," my recollection of which was to give me a clue to his subsequent "Fiona Macleod" mystification.

Of this, had I realized it at the time, I might have got an early hint from a conversation with Mrs. Sharp, during a visit to their country home, when, out for an evening walk, Sharp walking ahead with my wife, she told me that before long we should find "Will" coming out with some work richer and fuller than he had ever achieved before, the nature of which she must not at the moment confide. I watched for it, but a novel called "Silence Farm," though good, hardly seemed a fulfilment of Mrs. Sharp's forecast.

A short time after that I was spending the summer with Mr. and Mrs. Grant Allen in Surrey, and one morning the mail brought to Allen and me, to each of us, a copy of a little book called "Pharais," by a new writer—"Fiona Macleod." Grant Allen, among whose many great and endearing gifts was a genius for welcoming all novelties of promise, was enthusiastic, and immediately wrote one of his eager appreciations for, I think, the *Westminster Gazette*. But, before I wrote my review of it for my weekly article in the *Star*, I had made, or thought I had made, a discovery. Sharp was an intimate friend of both of us, and I said to Allen, "I'll bet you anything that 'Fiona Macleod' is no one else but—William Sharp." My reason for thinking so was that I had found "Fiona Macleod" using a description of the eerie sound made by the wind blowing over ice identical with lines which had powerfully struck me in one of those "Romantic Ballads" by William Sharp. The image was too striking to be a coincidence. Either Miss Macleod was plagiarizing or William Sharp was masquerading as Fiona Macleod. And this I proceeded to write in my article.

No sooner was the article published than I received

a telegram from Sharp saying: "For God's sake, shut your mouth"—which I immediately did, and kept it shut through all the ensuing "boom" of the new Gaelic writer which came on fast and furious. Sharp followed his telegram by a letter, promising to explain it at our next meeting. This he did, apparently in the fullest confidence, under oath of secrecy, an oath which it has long been unnecessary to keep, as the secret has long been out, though the story still retains certain elements of mystery, for Sharp would appear to have been an incorrigible romancer, and it may well have been that he gave his explanation an added colour of romance for my benefit. At all events, there was a very beautiful lady in the story—Sharp once spoke of her as a "cousin"—under whose influence he found himself inspired to write stories and poems that were not within his own unaided power. It was not an ordinary collaboration, something much stranger than that, inexplicably "psychic" maybe. One thing was sure, that the lady was very beautiful, and that their romantic friendship resulted in—"Fiona Macleod." It sounds to-day as though his mysterious "cousin" was a sort of embodied "Patience Worth." Sharp once showed me a photograph purporting to be the lady, but I did not believe him, for I thought I recognized it as the portrait of someone else. Also he further mystified me by saying that "Fiona Macleod" was shortly coming to London, and that he intended to introduce her to three people only—George Meredith, Mr. W. B. Yeats, and myself. The introduction to me was never made, and I believe it was all just a part of Sharp's masterly game of hide-and-seek. Certainly, the way in which he kept it up was remarkable and must have entailed upon him infinite industry and ingenuity. Though I never met that beautiful *alter ego* I have several letters from her, which Sharp must have written himself, or got someone to write—one of which is here reproduced—and his personal letters to me are full of references to her, messages from her, accounts of their working on some new book together, which had a most deceiving air of veracity. Here are one or two extracts:

"I have only now seen your delightful article on Miss Macleod's book. It came most aptly, for Miss M. is at present in London *en passant*, and so I was able to show it to her a little while ago. . . . Good news from Elizabeth I am glad to say. But F.M. alas! is not well. A glimpse of her to-day was all that was possible but she will be in the South Coast for a time, and I shall go there for all next week. . . ."

"F. is well, and pleased deeply by the success of her last book—in which, at last, you will see far more of her than of her friend. . . ."

At that time I possessed a fine and rare edition of "Ossian," the father of modern Celticism, and Sharp was anxious to see whether it contained anything missing from his own copy. So he wrote me, "Do you cling to that 'Ossian' of yours? Is he a disposable piece of goods? If a *lady* asked you to negotiate, would you yield?" The "lady," I presume, was Fiona Macleod, and, as I was glad to make Sharp a present of the volume, it perhaps contributed a little towards inspiring that mysterious "dual personality."

The truth behind all this romantic mystification probably was that Sharp had inherited in a high degree from his Highland blood (intermixed with Scandinavian on his mother's side) that psychic sensitiveness

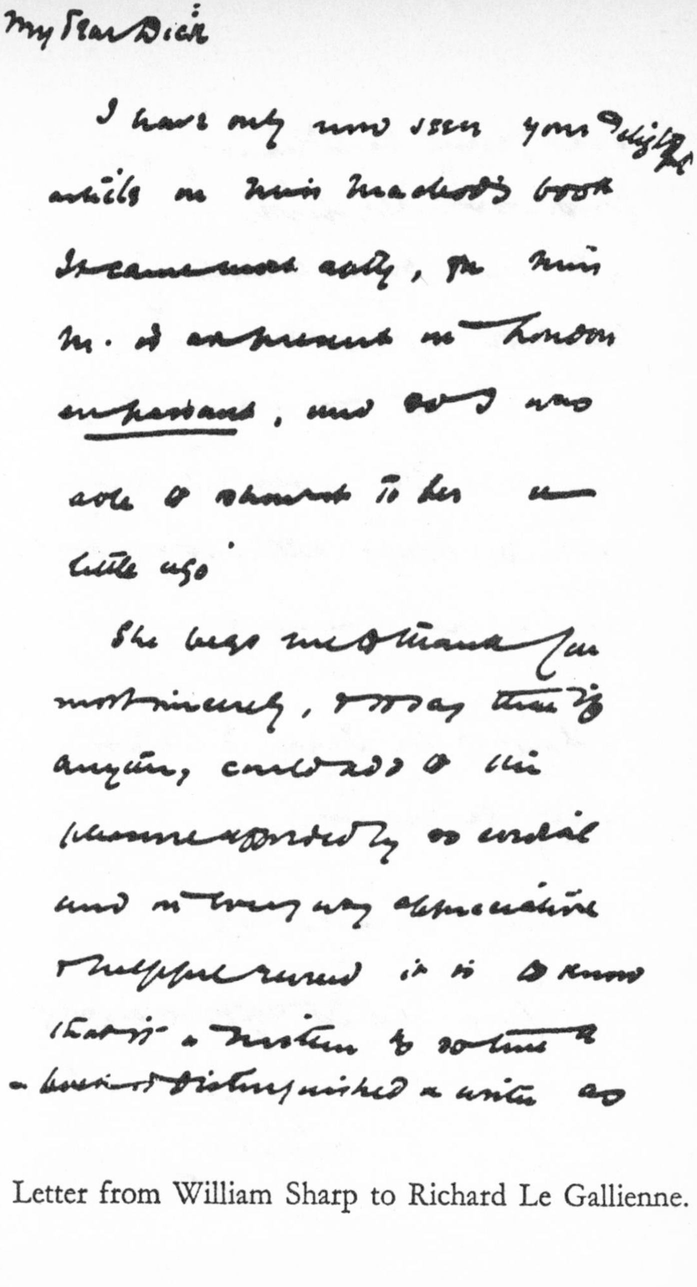
My dear Dick

I have only now seen your delightful article on Miss Macleod's book. It came somewhat early, for Miss M. is at present in London unexpectedly, and so I was able to show it to her a little ago.

She begs me to thank you most sincerely, & to say that if anything could add to the pleasure afforded by so cordial and in every way appreciative & helpful review it is to know that it is a tribute by so true & distinguished a writer as

Letter from William Sharp to Richard Le Gallienne.

...

Love to the dear Pilikin —
Your "Cousino" —

Ever, dear Wick,
Your friend affectionately

Wic

11th Augt 1899.

go. Miss Rea.
The Olimlia Literary Agency,
9. Mill St. Conduit St.
London. —

Dear Mr Le Gallienne
It was only a day or
two ago that I saw your most
friendly and sympathetic
notice of "The Dominion of
Dreams" — for I have been
yachting round the extreme
north of Scotland: and
though I have but a
snatched quarter of an
hour today to spare, for I

Letter from "Fiona Macleod" to Richard Le
Gallienne.

article I have seen & sent
me by our common friend)
— and hope that you will
publish the record in book-
form. I also greatly hope
for another volume of
poetry soon. You are a
poet first and foremost.
  Hurriedly but with most
  cordial greetings
     Sincerely yours
     Fiona Macleod.
     ———

which has often found manifestation in second sight. This, quickened by the friendship of a beautiful woman of spiritual and intellectual intuitions akin to his own, resulted in "Fiona Macleod." Such is the view of Mrs. William Sharp—than whom, of course, no one is in a better position to know the truth—who, in her admirable "Life" of her husband, identifies his muse as the lady to whom, under the initials of "E.W.R.," he dedicated the first "Fiona Macleod" romance *Pharais* (which is Gaelic for Paradise), in these words:

"There is another Paras than that seen of Alastair of Innisron—The Tir-Nan-Oigh of friendship. Therein we both have seen beautiful visions and dreamed dreams. Take then, out of my heart, this book of vision and dream."

Mrs. Sharp expressly identifies his friend as a lady whom her husband had met in Rome in 1893, and of whom he himself wrote to her—that is, Mrs. Sharp— "to her I owe my development as 'Fiona Macleod,' though, in a sense, of course, that began long before I knew her, and indeed while I was still a child . . . without her there would have been no 'Fiona Macleod.' "

Personal considerations apart, the whole story is of immense interest as illustrating the little known processes of artistic creation, for no one can compare the work written by William Sharp, under his own name, with that written by "Fiona Macleod" without being aware that some sort of "miracle" had taken place, for there is all the difference between something like genius and a not specially notable literary talent. Still, it is evident, too, that without William Sharp there would have been no "Fiona Macleod," for, William Sharp being dead, "Fiona Macleod" has vanished, too. Sharp's death at the early age of forty-nine, all too likely accelerated by the strain of his dual existence, which at one time, Mrs. Sharp tells us, threatened him with complete nervous collapse, was a peculiarly deep loss to his friends, for he was one of those personalities, so vital, so radiant, so charged with elemental fire and golden joyousness, that we can never conceive of their dying like other less animate people. As I have been looking through a great sheaf of his sun-filled letters, I cannot believe that they have not just come to me warm from the touch of his generous hand. But Sharp was far from being the only "too quick despairer" who departed prematurely from the scene in the '90s, for particularly in the case of the men who are in a special sense identified with that period, the men of *The Yellow Book*, The Rhymers' Club, and the Bodley Head, of whom I have now to write, early death seemed to be a *macabre* shadow taking part in the joyous spring dance of that *fin de siècle* renaissance. Perhaps it was because some of the dancers too zealously applied the counsel of the Master who bade them burn always with that hard gem-like flame. . . .

IV

I⊤ IS always as misleading as it is tempting to compress a period into a formula, and to find for it a "spirit" in which its expressive figures are supposed to participate, to bear the seal of it, so to say, upon their foreheads. In spite of the great diversity of personalities and ideals, social and artistic "messages" and "movements," that were so actively going their several ways in those many-coloured energetic years, "the '90s," are usually spoken of as if they had only one colour: the "yellow" '90s, or the "naughty" '90s, or the "decadent" '90s.

The Yellow Book has become the symbol of the period, and the two or three writers and artists to whom the word "decadence" may perhaps be applied have been taken as characteristic of a time which was far from being all "yellow," or "naughty," or "decadent." Even that group of writers most closely identified with this aspect of the '90s was only accidentally a group, and, being all of them strikingly independent individuals, had really very little in common. Indeed, when we examine their work, one might almost say that they had nothing in common but—a publisher. That publisher, however, was a remarkable one, no ordinary "Barabbas." We are so accustomed to regard authors and publishers as natural enemies that we forget that a publisher may occasionally be something like a creative artist. By his selective encouragement of new talents he may be instrumental in setting new fashions in literature, and by the general character of his business be no little of a contributory creator of taste. Such a creative publisher was John Lane, whose recent death has removed not merely one of the best-known figures of the '90s, but the man who was chiefly responsible for that phase of them with which, as we have said, they are popularly identified.

When Oscar Wilde went arrogantly to his trial in a lordly carriage and pair, he appeared on the witness stand with a copy of *The Yellow Book* under his arm, and he gave the name of "Lane" to a valet in one of his plays. This was because he didn't like Lane. Nor did Lane like him. Perhaps it was because they were both exceedingly smart business-men; for I remember Lane saying that though he disliked Wilde personally, such was the magic of his voice and the brilliancy of his conversation that he was afraid of transacting any business with him, because he was sure to be charmed into getting the worst of the bargain.

Lane was a remarkable man, and it is a great pity that he did not live to make that record of his recollections which I understand he contemplated, for no man knew so intimately the literary and artistic London of his day, and touched it at so many points. Lane was first of all a great collector, not only of books and pictures, but of furniture and indeed all kinds of charming collectable things. He was particularly proud of his collection of old glass, with which his rooms in the Albany were perilously crowded, so that one was afraid to turn about for fear of bringing some precious thing with a crash to the floor; particularly on those genial evenings when guests as heterogenous as the *objets d'art* which surrounded them would drop in for animated talk on their particular hobbies, with the usual humanizing accompaniments of tobacco and whisky-and-soda. Lane, too, used to give charming "teas," at which one met distinguished and beautiful women, dowagers, socialists, poets and artists—and among the latter I particularly recall the Rossetti-like head of Mrs. Graham R. Tomson, the boyish, bird-like charm of "E. Nesbit," the flower-like loveliness of Olive Custance—since Lady Alfred Douglas—and the noble silent beauty of Ethel Reed, whose early death robbed the world of a great decorative artist. At his masculine evenings one met, not merely writers and artists, but generals and literary lords who collected book-plates and old china, and venerable scholars mysteriously learned. Lane had great social tact, and usually these apparently incongruous figures were brought together because he was aware of mutual interests which would make them harmonious, and he always had some new "find" to exhibit, something picked up for a song in those old curiosity shops among which, like another Cousin Pons, he was continually on the prowl. His *flair* for such things was as unerring as his enthusiasm was almost child-like. Well do I remember nights when we have thus gone exploring together, returning home laden with various treasure trove which his keen eye had unearthed from most unpromising rubbish heaps of the past, and one evening in particular I recall when we reached the Albany, each with a Sheraton chair on his head, carrying our hats in our hands, oblivious of the amused passers-by.

It was the same *flair* and enthusiasm that Lane brought to literature. When I first knew him he was a clerk in a railway office near Euston, and I would sometimes meet him at the day's end and go on one of these expeditions. On one such occasion he told me that he had a friend in Exeter, named Elkin Mathews, who kept a bookshop in that city, and that he had influenced him to remove to London and set up business there. Soon after that a quaint little bookshop, with rare editions in its bay window, opened in Vigo Street, and before long a sign was swinging over the door with a painting of Sir Thomas Bodley on a panel. Such was the beginning of "Bodley Head," with Elkin Mathews, for a time, as its sole proprietor, though with Lane as its unseen *deus ex machina*. Mathews was a little man, as quaint as his shop, with a face not unlike the popular representation of "Punch." A gentle Lamb-like figure, he, too, was an ardent collector, and used particularly to pride himself on a cabinet which he believed had belonged to Izaak Walton—"Izaak Walton" being conspicuously carved on the front, a fact which shrewder collectors, such as Lane, considered as by no means confirming its vaunted association. Mathews had none of Lane's initiative and had been content to remain a bookseller, a specialist in "first editions"; but Lane's ambitious spirit prevailed, and their two names soon appeared together as publishers, their publishing business beginning modestly enough with a volume of bookish verses by the present writer, a volume whose sole distinction nowadays—though, of course, it was a heart-beating matter to me at the time—is, as I sometimes see in booksellers' catalogues, that it was "the first volume published at the Bodley Head"—a fact in which I take proper pride. Lane's pace was a little too fast for the Waltonian Mathews, and it was not long before they parted company, Lane taking the since famous sign to other premises across the street.

It was not long before the new publishing house with the quaint sign, like a tavern's, began to be talked about, particularly for two things. The books published by Lane were original and charming to look at. Lane had a genius for *format*, and his books had a new distinction and luxury about them. One knew a Bodley Head book at a glance. Lane was the first to apply to general publishing the new ideals in printing and binding that were already in the air, and which, before William Morris had started his Kelmscott Press, had found expression in such beautiful esoteric magazines as the *Century Guild Hobby Horse*, edited by Herbert P. Horne, Arthur Macmurdo and Selwyn Image, and the *Dial*, published under the joint editorship of Charles Ricketts and Charles H. Shannon, who were presently to start the Vale Press, one of the earliest of those "private presses" that were just then coming into fashion, and the most influential of them all. Lane had the advantages of the co-operation of Messrs. Ricketts and Shannon in several of his early volumes, notably in the exquisitely decorated editions of Father John Gray's "Silverpoints," "The House of Pomegranates," by Oscar Wilde, and the "Poems"of Lord De Tabley. There was a delightful aura of mystery about these early private presses, particularly about the Vale Press. Had Messrs. Ricketts and Shannon been alchemists, their operations could not have been veiled in a more thrilling secrecy, or the results awaited with more hushed expectancy; and specimen pages of any new book on which they were cloistrally engaged were shown privately by Lane to a favoured few as things sacrosanct, and occultly precious, with that reverent solemnity which characterizes

the true collector. The times were very serious about
Beauty.

The other thing that soon became known of Lane
and the Bodley Head was that he was strangely
desirous of publishing poetry, was willing even to pay
for it, and, moreover, was able to sell it. Till then
"the minor poet" had been a figure for newspaper
mockery, one of the favourite butts of *Punch*, which
indeed did no little to advertise the "Bodley Head
Poets" in the witty verses of Owen Seaman—since
also a knight—who sang of

> *A precious few, the heirs of utter godlihead*
> *Who wear the yellow flower of blameless bodlihead.*

We never hear of "minor" poets nowadays. Now,
when we are not "manifestly great" poets, we are at
least "authentic." And the removal of that stigma from
the poetic craft is largely due to Lane, who was able
to win newspaper respect for his poets—poets for
whose recognition he worked both as a friend as well
as a publisher. Of course, he had poets to work for,
who, whatever their size, were real, and, at all events,
of greater poetic energy than any who had appeared
since the days of Rossetti and Swinburne. At the same
time, these men would have had a far longer fight for
recognition had there been no Bodley Head; for the
difficulty of getting a volume of poems published up
till that time, unless the poet cared to pay the cost of it
himself, seems hard to believe to-day when poetry has
become so flourishing an industry.

There were not so many poets in the '90s as there
are nowadays, when indeed half the population of

the world seems to be made up of poets, and when, "joking apart," there is such a general high level of poetic achievement—a phenomenon likely to suggest to the profane that the writing of poetry is much easier than used to be supposed. But there were already a great number compared with the record of the preceding generation, so many indeed that England seemed once more a veritable "nest of singing-birds." William Archer turned aside from his militant dramatic criticism, which was one of the journalistic features of the time, and relaxed his usual austerity to appreciate thirty-three of them in his book "Poets of the Younger Generation." Archer put in a spirited protest against the term "minor poet." "Criticism," he said, "has made great play with the supercilious catchword 'minor poet.' No one denies, of course, that there are greater and lesser lights in the firmament of song; but I do most strenuously deny that the lesser lights, if they be stars at all and not mere factitious fireworks, deserve to be spoken of with contempt." This contempt, as Mr. Holbrook Jackson in his comprehensive and acute survey of the period has pointed out, carried with it a certain moralistic disapproval, implying an unbridled eroticism which was nothing like so characteristic of the poets of the '90s as it has been of the poets who have succeeded them. In fact, as I have said, these poets had very little in common, as will be seen by running one's eye over a list of the names most prominent then and not yet forgotten: Francis Thompson, Ernest Dowson, Lionel Johnson, John Davidson, Oscar Wilde, Arthur Symons, John Gray, Theodore Wratislaw, Olive Custance, "E. Nesbit," Graham R. Tomson (afterwards known as Mrs.

Marriott Watson), "Michael Field," Margaret L.
Woods, Ernest and Dollie Radford, William Watson,
Alice Meynell, A. E. Housman, Herbert Trench, W.
B. Yeats, Henry Newbolt, Rudyard Kipling, Victor
Plarr, Laurence Binyon, H. C. Beeching, F. B. Money-
Coutts, A. C. Benson, Sturge Moore, Selwyn Image,
Herbert P. Horne, Norman Gale, Stephen Phillips,
Lord Alfred Douglas, and Lord De Tabley.

Though the "free verse," "imagist," and general
anti-tradition poets of the moment, morbidly afraid of
"rhetoric" (in which they would seem to include
music) and fanatically insistent on every poet having
his own "individual accent," whether he himself is
possessed of a discernible individuality or not, poets
who would do much better to go to school to one of
the masters rather than attempt by wilful eccentricity
to "fake" a fictitious personality for themselves—
though these and their sympathetic critics would rele-
gate many of the poets in this list to the dustbin of
superannuated song, there is little doubt in the minds
of more catholic and central lovers of poetry that
several of them have come to stay, and that all of them
contributed something valuable to the general chorus.
Almost all these poets, including nearly all the best,
were fathered by the Bodley Head.

Among the names just cited the reader will have
noted the name of Lord De Tabley. He, too, was
among the "Bodley Head Poets," though it was somewhat surprising to find him *dans cette galère*, and his
presence there illustrates how inapplicable to them
was any comprehensive formula. Long known to a
few, a very few, lovers of poetry by distinguished
work of power as well as beauty which would have

made any other man famous, but which he did his best
to hide under a bushel, was he prompted by the Time
Spirit at length to emerge from his seclusion, or was it
that he had been accidentally gathered in by the wide
sweep of Lane's net? He was a shy, somewhat mysterious figure, who in time belonged to the older men of
the period, but who thus by his emergence into the
'90s comes to be associated with the younger generation. As far back as 1859 he had published a volume of
"Poems" under the pseudonym of "G. F. Preston,"
and in 1859 had published "Praeterita," by "William
Lancaster," and again in 1867 had published his fine
classical drama of "Philoctetes" under a third pseudonym "M.A." He seems to have had a perfect mania
for burying his work alive, and in 1868 published his
noble drama of "Orestes" once more under the pseudonym, "William Lancaster," under which name he
also wrote two or three unimportant novels. Only to
another volume of poems, "Rehearsals," in 1870,
did he append his real name, John Leicester Warren.
It was not surprising that, having taken such pains to
hush it up, so great a body of fine work remained
practically unknown. Indeed, such recognition as he
had received was in another field altogether, for
he was a learned botanist, and was one of the greatest
authorities on the not very popular study of brambles
in Europe. Therefore, when I first met him at one of
Lane's evenings, some knew him as a famous
"brambler," but outside a few men of his own generation, and a critic here and there such as Sir Edmund
Gosse, who has written a vivid and sympathetic
portrait of him, practically no one knew him as a poet.
I shall never forget the impression his wistful reserved

figure, as of a king in exile, made upon me that evening. There was something "hierarchical," too, about his noble head, with its longish rippled grey hair, and there was a curious mingling of gentleness and sympathy, with something almost of fierceness, in his melancholy but all-observant blue eyes. He was scarcely sixty, but he looked more like eighty as he sat there, with a detached, broken-spirited look, as of a fallen Saturn. He seemed like a man who had never recovered from some early sorrow, and I heard it mysteriously hinted that such was the case. He was the lord of a great estate in Cheshire, with a lovely old moated grange going back to the days of Richard II, preserved like a dream in the park of a later Tabley House, a vast Georgian structure, with memories of the Prince Regent; but he seldom visited this home of his fathers, preferring to live elsewhere.

At the time I met him certain of his friends had been endeavouring to arouse his ambition, with the suggestion that he should republish some of his old work. I was aware of this and ventured to urge him to do it, proposing that he should make a selection from his poems of what he considered best worth preserving. The idea seemed at once to please and alarm him. But he was such a poor judge of his own work, he said, and couldn't trust himself to know the good from the bad. Then, with an indescribable shyness, and as though he were asking me a preposterous favour, instead of, as I naturally felt, doing me a charming honour, he surprised me by saying that he would undertake it, if I would help him make the selections. Of course, I readily agreed, and thus I came to enjoy a measure of intimacy with him and gain some insight

into his lonely nature, so full of charming simplicity
and friendly humanity beneath its melancholy reserve.
Our work on the selections entailed many meetings,
and more letters, of which I possess a veritable stack.
We would take volume by volume, each make our
independent selections, and then compare them. There
was also a quantity of new work to go through. The
deference of that learned man to my humble opinion
was touching, almost embarrassing indeed at times. A
more gracious humility of nature—a rare thing indeed
among poets—it is impossible to imagine, and I was
constantly afraid of my own criticisms, because he was
always sure immediately to accept them as the last
word. In one of his letters he pathetically says: "I have
been so out of touch for many years with modern
verse-writing, that it would have been imprudent for
me in the highest degree to have meditated a reprint
without having a younger mind to consult." He had a
quaint way of dividing his tentative lists of selections
into what he called "dustbins," labelling them, according to his idea of their relative excellence, as *Dustbin I*
and *Dustbin II*. Thus he would write: "This is merely
to enclose *Dustbin the Second* mentioned yesterday. On
the whole 'Suckling' and 'The Spider' seem to me the
most promising items of the cargo, but this you can
judge better than I can." Again: "You have seen so
many of my failures that it will not make things worse
if you see some more. And if by any happy accident
any of the 5 could just scrape over the admission level,
it would be most acceptable just now. It is rather a
forlorn hope I know whether any of these 5 unpublished
pieces would do. Still One might, though I don't
expect it." And once more: "*Regret*. I am interested

to see you have hesitated over this as I have. Except the 'Madrigal' no piece has given me so much difficulty in deciding upon. With much hesitation I have included it—mainly because Matthew Arnold liked it." Of some new material, however, he writes in this unwontedly spirited fashion: "I find I have developed, as to this new material, after having been quite free from it in the old, that kind of obstinacy which affects, I suppose, at times even the humblest verse-writer. I care very little how I alter a piece which I have written 20 years ago or more. It seems like the work of another man. . . . But I am sorry to say that with a piece which I have recently written this process of cutting out and altering is exceedingly painful. . . . Had I written them long enough to forget them, I would hack at them and cut their throats, bleed them to death, and generally Whitechapel them without the smallest remorse." As will be seen from this, this work of selection was to him something like the travail of a new birth. However, the pangs were at last over, and when the volume appeared, with a remarkable *fin de siècle* cover by Mr. Charles Ricketts, its reception was so immediately and unanimously cordial as quite to dazzle with pleasure one who had been so long, and so deliberately, a recluse. It seemed to endow him with renewed youth, and I am happy to think I had a hand in bringing about that Indian summer of his fame.

Knowing that Lord De Tabley was interested in Hazlitt, I dedicated to him a reprint of the "Liber Amoris" which I had at that time edited. His letter in response will have such great interest for lovers of Hazlitt, and seems also so illuminative of De Tabley himself, that I believe the reader will thank me for printing it here. It will not be without interest, too, I imagine, to followers of the fashionable Freudian philosophy.

"I have, as you know, a strong *personal* interest in Hazlitt. Many better and more blameless men have failed to interest me as much. Coleridge is abler no doubt, but I don't care a brass halfpenny about him, as apart from two or three lyrics. Indeed, at times I loathe him. And, having this personal interest, I accept the complete and inexcusable Hazlitt, failings and all, and I could not do without the 'Liber Amoris,' tho' full of faults, vulgarities, absence of humour, and all you note. Still it is an honest record of a genuine and overpowering *infatuation*. We could not do without the Shakespeare sonnets, but the greatest of men plays in them a most unworthy part in this earlier Southampton infatuation. Well, I believe that no men with the note of minority in their work have ever suffered from these infatuations. I believe they seldom come till 40 is past, being quite apart from the superficial attractions of youthful sexual passion. I believe they come at first sight, and are quite apart from attachments of gradual knowledge, juxtaposition and opportunity. I fancy they reveal in theological language some great mystery, and reach the very taproots of our personality ; or, if you prefer to express this in terms more acceptable to the Royal Society (1893), they indicate an elemental instinct seldom reached except in men of the highest attainments. In this view, what the woman is matters absolutely nothing. The man supplies the play and the candles and draws up his own curtain. I need hardly say that I am one of those who think far better of Hazlitt for having suffered these things. And

I agree with you that all his Haymarket adventures of his earlier days can hardly have touched the surface of his nature, if at 40 he was capable of laying himself and his talents, regardless of consequences, at the feet of a shallow and mercenary maid-servant. W. B. Scott, with whom in the old days I used to discuss the 'Liber,' would have it that this love began in the sense of condescension and patronage which Hazlitt's position as Sarah's master gave Hazlitt. I disagree *toto caelo* from this. But Scott was an able man and his view should, now he is gone, be respected. I shall now read the text of the 'Liber' again. Your reprint has made me wish to do this. It has given a freshness to the subject, and has revived a half-faded rose."

"The Book of the Rhymers' Club," published by Lane in 1892, may be regarded as the first concerted attack of the "Bodley Head Poets" on the British public, though it was not conceived as such and had no prevailing tone. It had no purpose beyond bringing together in friendly association, after the manner of such old miscellanies as "England's Helicon" or Davison's "Poetical Rhapsody," examples of the work of twelve poets, most of them young and recently arrived in London, who had constituted themselves a very informal club which met casually, at odd times, at the houses of one or other of them, or at Doctor Johnson's old tavern, The Cheshire Cheese in Fleet Street, for discreet conviviality, conversation on literary matters, and the reading of their own new-born lyrics. It had none of the propagandizing significance of other such clubs of poetic revolutionaries before or since, and, as a body, was not an energetic institution, nor of long life. Its members lacked any common fusing artistic ideal such as has animated, say, the subsequent imagist movement. Each was doing his own work in his own way, and the significance of the club was in its individuals rather than in any collective character. Several of these chanced to be poets who were to become representative of their period, initiators of certain of its poetic trends, and the volume contained poems by them which have attained at least the tentative immortality of anthologies. The names of the twelve who contributed to the first "Book of the Rhymers' Club" (for it was followed by a second) alphabetically are: Ernest Dowson, Edwin J. Ellis, G. A. Greene, Lionel Johnson, Richard Le Gallienne, Victor Plarr, Ernest Radford, Ernest Rhys, T. W. Rolleston, Arthur Symons, John Todhunter, W. B. Yeats. I have not the book by me, but I am under the impression that printed in it, or in the second volume, for the first time were Dowson's "Cynara," Lionel Johnson's "By the Statue of King Charles at Charing Cross," Mr. Yeats's "Innisfree," and Mr. Plarr's "Epitaphium Citharistriae." As Mr. Plarr's whimsical "Epitaphium" is even yet less known than it deserves to be, and as it is characteristically "1890" in its mood, I will indulge myself by quoting it:

> *Stand not utterly sedately*
> *Trite oblivious praise above her!*
> *Rather say you saw her lately*
> *Lightly kissing her last lover.*
> *Whisper not "There is a reason*
> *Why we bring her no white blossom,"*
> *Since the snowy bloom's in season*
> *Strow it on her sleeping bosom:*

Oh, for it would be a pity
To o'erpraise her or to flout her:
She was wild, and sweet, and witty—
Let's not say dull things about her.

Dowson's "Cynara," again, would, I suppose, be
considered even more characteristically "1890." Certainly no poem is more associated with the period, and
perhaps of all the poems then written it is the one still
found most often to-day on the lips of youth. I remember well hearing Dowson recite it, fresh from his pen,
on one of those nights at The Cheshire Cheese. He was
a frail appealing figure, with an almost painfully sensitive face, delicate as a silverpoint, recalling at once
Shelley and Keats, too worn for one so young, hag-
gard, one could not but surmise, with excessive
ardours of too eager living. A charming, affectionate
high-strung nature, capable at times of strange frenzies
of excitement, deeply spiritual, and sensuous, too, as
such natures usually are, he was of those who passed
untimely from the scene, finding peace at last like
others of his generation, "too avid of earth's bliss," in
the bosom of the Catholic Church. I have a letter by
me from Lionel Johnson in which he refers to "my
dearest friend Dowson: who is now, *Laus Deo*, a
Catholic."

Lionel Johnson himself, prevailing ascetic though he
was, was another of those brief and brilliant figures of
the time that followed each other so swiftly to the
grave: Hubert Crackanthorpe, Aubrey Beardsley, John
Davidson, Stephen Phillips. Fragile creature as Johnson was, his was perhaps the most definite personality
of them all, the one that I can most clearly visualize,

standing out in lonely relief more firmly as time goes on. My first meeting with him gave me that surprise which everyone experienced who saw him for the first time. It was a Rhymers' Club evening held at the house of Mr. G. A. Greene. Only three or four of us had as yet dropped in, and were standing about discussing some knotty question of the poetic art, when a boy of fifteen or so, as it seemed, leaning alone against the fireplace, a son perhaps, I had thought, of our host, suddenly struck into the conversation with a mature authority and an unmistakably Oxford accent, and continued to talk with an array of learning that put the rest to silence.

"Who the devil is that youngster!" I asked.

"Why, don't you know!" was the answer, with bated breath. "Why, that is Lionel Johnson!"

Fresh from provincial Liverpool, how was I to know?—though I had heard of the recent advent in town of a young prodigy of learning, whose name was now brought back to me. There was always some Phoenix just come up from Oxford in those days, as probably there is still. I looked with wonder at the young scholar, who, it proved, was but a year younger than myself, being twenty-three. Not an advanced age, indeed, but not even the knowledge that he was Lionel Johnson could make him look more than fifteen, and he never seemed to look older as long as he lived, which was only two years longer than his friend Dowson, for he died when he was but thirty-five. His little, almost tiny, figure, was so frail that it reminded one of that old Greek philosopher who was so light of weight that he filled his pockets with stones for fear the wind might blow him away. It was hard to believe that such knowledge and such intellectual force could be housed in so delicate and boyish a frame.

As I recall him, his face had no little resemblance to De Quincey's, though it was finer, keener, more spiritual. When I first knew Joyce Kilmer he reminded me very much of Johnson, with his then thin, austere young face and strangely strong and gentle eyes, eyes that seemed to have an independent, dominating existence. Johnson's eyes were like that, too, and his very concentrated, intense young presence had an amazing carrying power. But beneath his ascetic intensity, and behind that battery of learning, there was a deep and warm and very companionable humanity, as my subsequent friendship with him was to discover. He had a genius for friendship, and no man was ever more devoted and loyal to his friends. By the end of that evening Johnson and I seemed to have known each other for years, and as he lived in Gray's Inn, and I in Staple Inn near by, he proposed our walking home together. As we neared my domicile he proposed, the night being still young, that I should repair with him to his rooms for a final libation, and, as we mounted his stairs, he made a remark which makes me smile as I write, for it was very "1890."

"I hope you drink absinthe, Le Gallienne," he said, "for I have nothing else to offer you."

Absinthe! I had just heard of it, as a drink mysteriously sophisticated and even Satanic. To me it had the sound of hellebore or mandragora. I had never tasted it then, nor has it ever been a favourite drink of mine. But in the '90s it was spoken of with a self-conscious sense of one's being desperately wicked, suggesting diabolism and nameless iniquity. Did not Paul Verlaine drink it all the time in Paris!—and Oscar Wilde and his cronies, it was darkly hinted, drank it nightly at the Café Royal. So it was with a pleasant shudder that I watched it cloud in our glasses, as I drank it for the first time, there alone with Lionel Johnson, in the small hours, in a room paradoxically monkish in its scholarly austerity, with a beautiful monstrance on the mantelpiece and a silver crucifix on the wall.

As I looked at his almost diaphanous frame, I could not help even then thinking that absinthe was too fierce a potion for one so delicately made, so lacking in protective phlegm; but that Johnson was in any real danger never, of course, occurred to me, and the day was yet far off when he was to make that tragic end in Fleet Street, stupidly knocked down by a hansom cab, when, poor fellow, his good wits were not all, for the moment, at his service. A drunkard, in the ordinary sense, or even "a drinking man," Johnson was not and could never have been. Probably Johnson, like too many men who work with their brains, not all poets, had been tempted to risk that dangerous experimentation with alcohol, because, particularly in the form of his favourite absinthe, it has for a time so quickening and clarifying an effect on the intellectual and imaginative faculties. But he was weak of body, and the thing was stronger than he. It was, I am convinced, but a passing phase with him, and but for that fatal accident, his firm will would undoubtedly have prevailed. He was sincerely religious, too, and, as we have seen in the case of Dowson, while, of course, no proselytizer, was solicitous for the spiritual safety of his friends and anxious that they should find refuge where he himself had found it. After his death I was touched by coming upon in a bookseller's catalogue a copy of my own "Religion of a Literary Man" in which he had written this prayer for the safety of my soul: *Sancte Thomas Aquinas, per orationes tuas in ecclesiam Christi trahe scriptorum amicum meum.*

Johnson was an exquisite letter-writer, and I wish that a volume of his letters could be brought together. Perhaps that will some day be done. Meanwhile the reader will like to see this beautiful letter, characteristically written on the subject of his "learning." It was *à propos* his book on Thomas Hardy, which some critics considered overladen with erudition.

20 FITZROY STREET

Thursday

MY DEAR LE GALLIENNE,

Very many thanks for your kind and welcome praises of my book; they are refreshing, after the somewhat savage, and slightly silly, utterances of our friend, the *Chronicle*. What do these dear people mean by "learning"? Some of my critics while saying pleasant and cordial things, yet raise hands of amazement at my "learning," or bend brows of reproach at my "pedantry." And yet I am neither learned, nor pedantic, but simply fond of literature. It is as natural to me to quote Aristotle, or Æschylus, as to quote Stevenson, or Bridges, just because I like them: but I begin to believe, I must be lean, pale, spectacled, stooping, bent over dusty folios, great at Arabic, and hating frivolity. It must be a dream, that I love walking tours, whisky, dogs, the Alhambra, and a joke. Seriously, I am the poorest of scholars: to take the Oxford test, I got a first in "Greats," but a bad second in "Mods." I read the classics, and foreign literatures, for mere love of them: my memory is good, and when I sit down to write, quotations pour in upon me; Pascal jostling Mr. Sims, Goethe tumbling over Zangwill, Cicero elbowing John Morley. I was lately walking at the Land's End, and found myself, unconsciously declaiming Virgil and Arnold to the seagulls. And this perfectly natural instinct, neither a merit, nor a fault, is put down, as laborious and affected pedantry. One would think, a writer were bound to apologize, should he dare mention an author of more than fifty years since: and that, if he do so dare, it must be the result of painful research. No one ever reproaches an architect, painter, musician, for being decently acquainted with the history and triumphs of his art: it is only natural, that he should be. Doubtless, I overdo quotation: but it is from mere exuberance of delight, not in any spirit of pedantry. How can one help knowing things so delightful, or making use of them? I won't say, that my reproachful critics are ignorant, but, assuredly, I am not learned. I will only say, that they do not know what learning is: I do.

"Casual commas": I thank you: no, you are right, my commas, Heaven be praised, are *not* casual. What right has anything, in any work of art, however slight, to be casual? Oh, for the scholarly graces of Addison and Goldsmith!

But, my dear Le Gallienne, I did not mean to inflict upon you this harangue. *Vivas: Floreas: Valeas;*

ever yours,

LIONEL JOHNSON.

Was the joyous soul of the scholar ever put into words with more convincing charm?

Someone has said that the '90s was a time of "little giants." The expression is a good one, and the man whom perhaps it especially fits was John Davidson, whose personality was rocky and stubborn and full of Scotch fight, with no little of Scotch pig-headedness. But with him, as with the lion in Holy Writ, within whose jaws the wild bees built their honeycombs, it was a case of *ex forte dulcedo*: for beneath his proud, rather pragmatic exterior, and that Highland manner which brings a suggestion of always going armed against offence, his nature was full of human kindness and repressed tenderness. His life was hard from boyhood, and even when recognition of his gifts came to him, he continued, at least, to regard it as hard, because he found, as many another poet has done, that fame was more cry than wool, and that earning his livelihood continued as difficult as ever. In this he was really no worse off than several of his famous contemporaries, but he had no bend in him, would not, or could not, stoop to journalism. A poet who insisted on reality in his work, he was incapable of adapting himself to those materialistic conditions with which the most inspired poet must compromise if he is to continue to exist. His consciousness of genius made him unpractically scornful of the doubtless exasperating limitations of "the nation of shopkeepers" among whom his lot was cast, and his sense of grievance, rather inflamed than mitigated by a yearly pension of one hundred pounds from the far from inexhaustible Royal Literary Fund, grew into a permanent grudge against society and gave a Nietzschean ferocity to the "Testaments" in which towards the close of his life he laboured to shatter it to bits and remould it nearer to the heart's desire. Then he had bad luck with the theatre, the plays which he wrote or adapted for Mrs. Campbell, Forbes-Robertson and Beerbohm-Tree gaining little more than an artistic success. These disappointments and the threat of cancer were eventually too much for his endurance, and he ended his life by throwing himself into the sea from the cliffs of Penzance in Cornwall, his body not being found till six months afterwards, and then, according to his wish, buried at sea. In a tragically outspoken preface to his last book of poems "Fleet Street and Other Poems" he had given this warning: "The time has come to make an end. There are several reasons. I find my pension is not enough; I have therefore still to turn aside and attempt things for which people will pay. My health also counts. Asthma and other annoyances I have tolerated for years; but I cannot put up with cancer." Cancer is perhaps a sound and terrible argument, but, at the same time, to attack society and to expect it to support us, as others besides John Davidson have done, is at least unphilosophical.

My emigration to America prevented my knowing Davidson in this last dark period of his life. My intimacy with him covered only the years of transient brightness when, after a long grind at schoolmastering in Scotland, he came up to London in 1890, definitely to embrace a literary career. He had already published one or two plays without success, particularly his brilliant fantastic pantomime "Scaramouch in Naxos," as well as a remarkable prose romance "Perfervid," both of which ought to be republished, and in 1891 he published a volume of poems called "In a Music Hall," which made the critics aware of him, paving the way for the enthusiastic reception in 1893 of his "Fleet Street Eclogues," which I had the honour of accepting for Lane. It was through this book that I came to know him, and his recognition of such service as I was able to do him in the newspapers was as generous and wholehearted as it was unusual. I remember with gratitude that when there was a concerted attack upon me and my "log-rolling" propensities, which lasted no less than a fortnight in the *Westminster Gazette*—to me a joyous and exhilarating all-in-the-day's work experience—Davidson stood manfully by me, and I quote a letter he sent me on the occasion—rather personal though it is—as an example of his energetic fighting spirit, as well as of his chivalrous loyalty to a friend.

20 PARK RIDINGS, HORNSEY, N.
29 *January*, 1895.

MY DEAR LE GALLIENNE,

I had no idea until to-day, as I dropped my brief connection with a press-cutting agency a fortnight ago, that the log-rolling logomachy had assumed such proportions, and hurtled with such prodigious theatrical thunder about your ambrosial locks. Of course you would never deem me so wanting in regard for you as to suspect me of suggesting sympathy in any such connection, but I thought you might care to know how I also have been somewhat amazed, not a little amused, and finally altogether "scunnered" by the pertinacity, the utter unintelligence, and bitter venom of these impotent and inept scribblers, who, having nothing in them deserving praise, are utterly unable to comprehend the laudable in others, whether it be the capacity of producing that which merits applause, or the rarer capacity of bestowing exquisite commendation on the works of their friends and enemies: in both capacities I might ask you to tell Narcissus some have considered that he excels. It hardly becomes me to say even this much, because until Narcissus struck the flint there was no welcoming fire anywhere for me, and yet even for that reason it more than becomes me to say how much I admire him and the lonely appreciative height where he stands barked at by scavenging dogs of depreciation.

Yours ever,

JOHN DAVIDSON.

On an impulse have sent gist of this to *Westminster* for publication.

So John Davidson, at all events, stood the test suggested by Mr. George Moore: "All very charming indeed . . . but why not in a newspaper?"

Davidson once sent me a couplet running:

What is between us two we know:
Shake hands, and let the whole world go—

which appeared afterwards in a dedication "To my Friend," accompanied by this delightfully savage dedication "To my Enemy":

Unwilling friend, let not your spite abate,
Feed me with scorn, and strengthen me with hate.

When my wife died, Davidson sent me the little poem which I reproduce here in facsimile, both as a

M. L. G.

Where do the dead folk go?
Where is this white soul glowing
Serene and sweet?
How shall we rest, not knowing?
How can we know?
And shall we meet,
Where the dead folk do go?

What of the darkness? Ah! he sang it well,
And now he needs his song.
But this — we cling to this, however long
In Time's dark night we dwell:
A lamp of life once lit not Death itself can
                                quell.

Our songs are sweeter far,
The flowers about our feet
Sweet and more sweet,
And every star
Is starrier,
Because of her.
                    John Davidson

Poem by John Davidson.

sample of his hand-writing and for its own sake. His was a noble nature, and his death was a real loss to literature, as well as to his friends, for he was in stature perhaps the biggest of all the poets of the '90s, and had in him the greatest potentialities of a many-sided genius, at once poetic, dramatic, and fantastic. His "Ballad of a Nun"—with such unforgettable lines as

I am sister to the mountains now,
And sister to the sun and moon—

had a larger accent than any other poems of his time, as his "Fleet Street Eclogues" had a spontaneous loveliness in its rural pictures such as will be found nowhere else. In his combination of modern realism with beauty, the apprehension of beauty, that is, in contemporary realities, as in his note of revolt against conventional hypocrisies, and his vindication of the free play of human vitality, he was expressive of the best energies and ideals of the 1890 Renaissance.

V

THOUGH, as I have said, the poets of the '90s were all
distinct individualities, doing their own work in their
own way, with no common artistic aims or pro-
grammes, they, of course, as usually happens in every
period, showed in some degree the influence of the
general revolutionary Time Spirit, and in two or three
cases, indeed, proved to be independently working
on the same lines. This is especially true of the revival
of interest in the town and urban things. Several of
them seem to have awakened simultaneously to the
poetry of London, and in prose as well as in verse there
was, for a time, quite a cult of London and its varied
life, from costers to courtesans. A generation before,
Robert Buchanan had written his "London Poems"
(1866) and of greater influence was Rossetti's "Jenny,"

> *Lazy laughing languid Jenny,*
> *Fond of a kiss and fond of a guinea,*

and this, doubtless, in addition to his Paris affiliations,
had its influence on Mr. Arthur Symons with his
celebration of the music-hall, and his Noras of the
Pavement. Then there was W. E. Henley with his
"London Voluntaries," among the earliest experi-
ments in "free verse." John Davidson, as we have
seen, had published a volume entitled "In a Music
Hall," and, particularly in his "Fleet Street Eclogues,"
he had sung with rare freshness the beauty of both
town and country. But none of the 1890 poets had
more deliberately set himself to express modern

London in verse than Stephen Phillips, though that earlier endeavour of his was rather lost sight of in the great success of his later poetic dramas. It was through this shared interest—for I, too, touched by the Time Spirit, had written "A Ballad of London" and "the iron lilies of the Strand"—that Stephen Phillips and I came to know each other. He wrote me a letter, *à propos* that ballad, confiding his own aims in that direction, which is of general interest as showing how the wind was blowing with him as with others. In it he says:

"You may have come across a poem of mine, 'Christ in Hades,' which has attracted some considerable attention." (It had, indeed, won a prize of one hundred pounds from the review called the *Academy*, as being the best poem of the year.) "I thought I should like to write to you. I was talking to Mr. Lane the other day about modern poetry and was saying that I felt sure that the new poetry must grapple with and depict the life of to-day. One gets sick of these eternal echoes more or less cleverly caught. I was saying to Mr. Lane that it was the ambition of my life to try and win something out of modern existence, and I mentioned a poem of yours which I had very greatly admired. It is called 'A Ballad of London.' Now if you will excuse my impertinence, why do we not have more of these? You seem to have got at the very heart of the Strand, and though one may take exception to one or two lines, the execution seems most happy. I thought perhaps you would not take it amiss if I wrote and said what I thought, and as I am now continually working on such themes, my opinion is not utterly worthless. I have got one or two subjects out of

London which I think might interest you. The Lead-Worker, the lead in her body in conflict, say, with a child in her womb. Has Dante ever conceived anything more terrible than these quite ordinary episodes in the life of the London worker? But I will not bore you further. Only I know that a word of 'sympathy' is so much to me and thought I should like to write to you. Might one hope now and then for some sympathy from you in a task which is I know dear to you—the poem of modern life. I send you a little ballad somewhat modern and grim which you may like, also a poem called 'A Dead Woman.' You know how absolutely dead many of these women look, as though they had survived their souls—yet how neatly they go about—the chief horror perhaps."

The poem referred to is, of course, "The Woman with the Dead Soul," a piece of imaginative realism still unsurpassed in its conveyance of the ghastliness of the living-dead, and the poet's terror at the comely apparition of the really "dead woman" whom he saw one day sewing in a London tavern:

Speckless, arrayed; and with no braid awry,
All smoothed and combed, she sewed incessantly . . .
Yet think how I stood mourning by the side
Of her who sat, but seemed as she had died;
Cold, yet so busy; though so nimble, dead;
Whose fingers ever at her sewing sped.
I spoke with her, and in slow terror guessed
How she, so ready for perpetual rest,
So smoothly combed and for the ground prepared,
Whose eyes, already fixed, beyond me stared,
Could sidle unobserved and safely glide
Amid the crowd that wist not she had died.

Another poem, "The Wife," the story of a woman who sells her body to buy food for her dying husband, is full of vivid London pictures, such as:

> *The joyous, cruel face of boys;*
> *These dreadful shadows proffering toys;*
> *The constable, with gesture bland,*
> *Conducting the orchestral Strand:*
> *A woman secretly distrest,*
> *And staidly weeping, dimly drest;*
> *A girl, as in some torment, stands,*
> *Offering flowers that burn her hands; . . .*
> *Creatures we marred, compelled upright*
> *To drift beside us in the light.*

The pitiful humanity, the clairvoyant imagination of these pictures, have a permanent value, not subject to fleeting fashions of taste. The '90s were surely not wrong in "crowning" such work. But these early successes, as I said, were soon to be half forgotten in Phillips's theatrical triumphs. One evening, as I was sitting in the stalls at the Haymarket Theatre, then under George Alexander's management, an usher came to me with a request from Mr. Alexander—not yet matured into knighthood—that I would step "behind" for a few moments. I was pleased to find that his business with me concerned Stephen Phillips. He wanted my opinion as to Phillips's possibilities as a playwright.

Did I think he had it in him to write a play? It was easy to answer that I considered Phillips's poetry unusually charged with dramatic imagination, and that, to my thinking, he was just the man to revive the poetic drama. Alexander then told me that he had it in mind to ask Phillips to write him a play on the story of Paolo and Francesca. A day or two afterwards, Phillips called in to see me with the exciting news that he had just got the commission. The play was not produced till three years after, and, meanwhile, Beerbohm-Tree had produced his "Herod" with great *éclat*. Phillips had one great advantage over many political dramatists, that of having been an actor himself. At the end of his first term at Cambridge, his cousin, Mr. F. R. Benson came there with his Shakespearean company, and Phillips persuaded him to give him a trial on the stage. The result was that he acted for six years, playing, among other parts, Flute in "A Midsummer Night's Dream," Gremio in "The Taming of the Shrew," the Duke in "Othello," and the Ghost in "Hamlet." It probably pleased him to recall that Shakespeare is traditionally said to have excelled in the part of the Ghost, and the part was so much to Phillips's liking that, after his success as a poet, he played it again with Sir Martin Harvey in 1905. I can well imagine him in it, for he had a very fine voice, and read his own poetry with great impressiveness. He had, too, a very striking presence, being tall and well built, and his clean-shaven face, with its strong regular features, was markedly "classical." His eyes particularly struck me by their curious piercing gaze, with that look in them suggesting clairvoyance. He was, indeed, somewhat inclined to "psychic" experiences, and once told me about seeing the ghost of his mother; a recollection which recalls another not quite so dread in its import.

Phillips, in spite of his rather solemn blank-verse

manner, was very much of a human being, a notable boon companion, and I am far from regretting that we often heard the chimes at midnight together in the old city we both loved so well. However, it was in broad daylight that the ghostly incident I am thinking of took place. At the close of an afternoon spent together "at the Mermaid," I walked with him to his train at Waterloo Station, for he lived an hour's run out of town. On Waterloo Bridge we encountered a pretty young woman, with whom, it must be confessed, we had enjoyed no previous acquaintance. She, however, being apparently willing to waive that conventionality, made no objection to our interviewing her about the weather or some such harmless subject, after which we went on our way, and I presently saw Phillips safely off on his train. A day or two afterwards Phillips called in, and, with much gravity, told me his curious sequel. On reaching home he had found his wife in a gloomy and not very welcoming mood. Phillips tried for some time, but vainly, to discover what was wrong. To all his anxious inquiries she answered that there was "Nothing." However, at last, to his amazement, she faced him with the question:

"Who was the girl you spoke to on Waterloo Bridge before you caught the train?"

Denials were vain, for presently Mrs. Philips described our chance acquaintance with great particularity, giving femininely exact details of her clothes, the style of her coat, the shape and trimmings of her hat, etc. . . . So there was nothing to be done but to own up, for it was evident that she had "seen" us all there together on the bridge. Mrs. Phillips will not, I am sure, mind my recalling this curious example of wifely clairvoyance, so striking an illustration, too, of Stevenson's well-known remark that "to marry is to domesticate the Recording Angel."

When Phillips was playing the Ghost with Sir Martin Harvey, Oscar Wilde, who loved the atmosphere of the theatre, and liked to sit of an evening talking witty nonsense in the dressing-rooms of his friends, dropped in now and again to see him; and Phillips told me how one evening he surveyed him with his elaborate serio-comic gravity and said, in his cadenced voice, and with his usual long pauses between each word, which he let fall with immense unction, as though he were carefully setting them in their places in an invisible pattern on the air: "Ah! Stephen—my—sins—are of—scarlet—and purple— but your sins—are—of white—marble!" It was an utterance characteristic not only of Wilde but of the period. Wilde was always half-humorously talking of "purple sins"; and "sin" as a developing factor in personality played a great part in the fashionable *blague* of all the would-be decadents, who loved to pose as mysteriously wicked. To *épater la bourgeoisie* is still, as it has always been, one of the artless pastimes of artistic youth, but in a certain circle in the '90s it was something like a gospel. The opportunities for shocking were greater then than now, when very little is left to do in that way.

A typical story was told me by a hard-worked editor, himself well known for his wit. One evening, as he was standing on a subway platform waiting for a train, work-weary from a busy day, a certain young poet, not unknown, came up to him in an excited manner and, button-holing him, said:

"My dear——, I am so happy—I've just got tangled up with a married woman!"

Now the poor editor had a wife, as was common knowledge among his friends, who was very much of a termagant, a hard-featured, generally unattractive woman of grenadier build, who made his life anything but a bed of roses; and, looking down with a sad smile on his callow young friend, he retorted, with a readiness born of much bitter experience:

"God bless my soul! I've been that for twenty years!"

That young poet's delightfully absurd remark was symptomatic of what to some degree was a genuine and serious revolt against Victorian conventionalities, and even moral standards, which the times in every direction were actively undermining. Though, of course, it had its foolish, and even its dangerous, sides, there was real, and indeed inevitable, change behind it. Many and various currents of thought had converged to bring it about, and particularly the teaching of such popularizers of evolutionary science as Huxley and Tyndall. The theological conceptions of our fathers had suffered serious disintegration, and the social sanctions and restrictions founded upon them were rapidly losing their authority. A larger and deeper spirituality, a more human morality, in which the influence of Walt Whitman counted for much, was breaking the old moulds and making for a freer exercise of vital emotions and functions than had been considered proper, or had been even possible before. The senses were beginning outspokenly to assert their natural rights against the hypocritical prudery which had hushed them up, and by its artificial reticences outlawed them as forbidden and unmentionable. Swinburne's poetry of the "noble and nude and antique," with its battle cry of

> *What ailed us, O gods, to desert you*
> *For the creeds that refuse and restrain?*
> *Come down and redeem us from virtue,*
> *Our Lady of Pain,*

had sunk deep, and much of the poetic revolt was directly inspired by him. Generally speaking, all authority founded on those narrow negations which had no warrant in reality were under fire. Pleasure was no longer being regarded as suspect, nor natural functions as evil; while all the social conventions founded on such arbitrary misinterpretations of human energy were under fire. All forms of authority, indeed, were challenged to stand and deliver. Women, too, were beginning to assert the right to a larger freedom, and in the relations of the sexes a new and wholesome camaraderie was beginning to obtain. In this the part played by the humble bicycle, which inaugurated a freer intercourse between men and women, should not be forgotten in any survey of the time. Younger people were no longer restricted to the frigid exchanges of the Victorian drawing-room, but were able to adventure together along country roads and wide commons, and fraternize humanly over intimate meals at country inns. The vote was not far off for women, and the typewriter girl was soon to invade the sacred precincts of masculine offices. The world was beginning to realize that work and duty were not everything, and that life was meant at least as much for play. I myself had written: "A New Spirit of Pleasure is abroad amongst us, and one that blows from no mere coteries of hedonistic philosophers, but comes on the four winds." Indeed, on the sadder side, perhaps the pessimism inherent in Fitz-Gerald's "Omar," the wide popularity of which was another symptom, was, in an age that had lost its old faiths, finding expression in a widespread application of the philosophy of *carpe diem*. Life was brief and uncertain, death was sure, and the future dark. Therefore, why not "gather ye rosebuds while ye may"? Otherwise burn always with that hard gem-like flame! In short, the '90s were generally sowing that wind of which we may be said to be now reaping the whirlwind.

All the various tendencies were summed up and accelerated by the plays of Oscar Wilde and Mr. Bernard Shaw, the drawings of Aubrey Beardsley, and *The Yellow Book*. How *The Yellow Book* came by its name I don't recall, but the choice of the colour yellow seems to have been a direct inspiration of the Time Spirit— otherwise, as some evidently felt, the devil; for the colour was very much in the air. I myself noted this at the time in a "prose fancy" on "The Boom in Yellow," in which, as Mr. Holbrook Jackson reminded me, I neglected to trace the decorative use of yellow to Whistler. I drew attention, however, to its wide employment by bill-posters and to Mr. Dudley Hardy's popular poster of "The Yellow Girl," and possibly I was near the mark in saying, *à propos* the previous "aesthetic" Burne-Jones cult of green, that "even the aesthete himself would seem to be growing a little weary of its indefinitely divided tones, and to be anxious for a colour sensation somewhat more positive than those to be gained from almost imperceptible nuances of green. Jaded with over-refinements and supersubtleties, we seem in many directions to be harking back to the primary colours of life. Blue, crude and unsoftened, and a form of magenta, have recently had a short innings; and now the triumph of yellow is imminent." "The Yellow Aster" was the title of a popular novel of the day, and Mr. A. C. Benson (whose fame as an essayist has unduly overshadowed his excellence as a poet) had actually anticipated the title of the famous magazine in his privately printed volume of poems called "Le Cahier Jaune." Indeed, that "boom in yellow" may well seem to have been prophetic of the coming triumph of "jazz" in all the arts, and particularly of the prismatic colouring of our modern painters. However it was, *The Yellow Book* certainly struck the psychological moment, and the shock which it gave the British public, with "its flaming cover of yellow, out of which the Aubrey Beardsley woman smirked at the public for the first time," was deep and lasting. As Mr. Holbrook Jackson has written: "Nothing like *The Yellow Book* had been seen before. It was newness *in excelsis*: novelty naked and unashamed. People were puzzled and shocked and delighted."

The Yellow Book was certainly novel, even striking, but, except for the drawings and decorations by Beardsley, which, seen thus for the first time, not unnaturally affected most people as at once startling, repellent, and fascinating, it is hard to realize why it should have seemed so shocking. But the public is an instinctive creature, not half so stupid as is usually taken for granted. It evidently scented something queer and rather alarming about the strange new quarterly, and thus it almost immediately regarded it as symbolic of new movements which it only partially represented. Even that compromise, which, after the first four or five numbers, was to rob it of any disquieting originality, was already present in the first issue. This was the shrewd Lane's doing. He was afraid to let its editors, Henry Harland and Aubrey Beardsley, be as daring as they wished to be, and so with such representatives of "modernity" as Max Beerbohm, Arthur Symons, George Egerton, Hubert Crackanthorpe, John Davidson, John Oliver Hobbes, and George Moore, he sandwiched in such safe and even "respectable" writers as Henry James, Arthur Christopher Benson, William Watson, Arthur Waugh, Richard Garnett, and Edmund Gosse, while he sought to break the shock of Beardsley with a frontispiece by Sir Frederic Leighton. The artists indeed were more "new and strange" than the writers, though there was certainly nothing to shock in the contributions by Laurence Housman, Joseph Pennell, Will Rothenstein, Walter Sickert and Charles Conder, whose lovely work is one of the most notable and lasting legacies of the 1890s. Poor Lane had a rather nerve-wracking time with Beardsley, who, for the fun of it, was always trying to slip some indecency into his covers, not apparent without close scrutiny, so that Lane used to go over them with a microscope and submit them to a jury of his friends before he ventured to publish. Even so, I remember that one issue had gone to press before a particularly audacious impropriety was discovered, with the result that the whole binding had to be cancelled. It was quite a game of hide-and-seek between Lane and Beardsley, in which Beardsley took a boyish delight.

1902

To Dicke

O witches by American trains!
Ram shirtle you brown in his fifes.
We love you for loving the stars,
That what can you see — the strifes?

Post Card from Max Beerbohm to
Richard Le Gallienne.

As for the literary contributions, though I do not have *The Yellow Book* to refer to, I do not think that the first volume contained anything more shocking than Davidson's "Ballad of a Nun"—which had, indeed, been rejected by the proprietor of *The Fortnightly Review* as "disgustingly licentious"—and Mr. Beerbohm's "A Defence of Cosmetics"—a piece of writing which to-day seems curiously prophetic of the lip-stick age which was soon to follow but had not yet arrived. However, it was Beardsley's strong personality that threw its "yellow" light over the whole, and in the first few numbers the compromising elements didn't count.

With Beardsley I had but a slight acquaintance, but I saw enough of him to realize his high intellectual gifts and the charm of his nature. Once I had an interesting talk with him about his romance "Under the Hill," and I recall the excitement with which he told me of some of the illustrations he proposed making, notably one of the wardrobe of Venus, with all its provocative garments. In such feminine matters he was as abnormally learned as he was in the curious byways of French and other classical literature. He was a strange, rather uncanny figure, spectrally lean and delicate, almost diaphanous, yet suggesting great nervous strength and energy. Oscar Wilde flashed him in a phrase to me one day as "a face like a silver hatchet, with grass-green hair," a description which his portrait of himself confirms. He was another of the "doomed" figures of the period, dying of consumption at the age of twenty-five, a devout Catholic, and begging his friends to destroy his "bawdy drawings." "By all that is holy, *all* obscene drawings," he wrote, adding after his signature "in my death agony." Collectors being what they are, it was scarcely to be hoped that they would heed that pathetic appeal. The story of Whistler's appreciation has been told before, but it is worth re-telling. Whistler had been originally prejudiced against his work, but when Beardsley showed him his illustrations to "The Rape of the Lock," he completely surrendered, saying with great deliberation: "Aubrey, I have made a very great mistake—you are a very great artist." The praise of the Master was too much for the young artist, and he burst into tears; and Whistler presently added, "I mean it—I mean it—I mean it." Everyone means it to-day, and his far-reaching influence has been incalculable.

With Henry Harland, the other editor of *The Yellow Book*, I enjoyed an affectionate intimacy. Harland was one of those Americans in love with Paris who seem more French than the French themselves, a slim, gesticulating, goateed, snub-nosed lovable figure, smoking innumerable cigarettes as he galvanically pranced about the room, excitedly propounding the *dernier mot* on the build of the short story or the art of prose. He was born to be the life and soul of one of those *cénacles*, which from their café-tables in "the Quarter" promulgate all those world-shaking "new movements" in art which succeed each other with kaleidoscopic rapidity. The most vivacious of talkers, "art" with him, as with his Parisian prototypes, was a life-and-death matter. Nothing else existed for him. He had no other interests. And, after all, why should an artist have any other? So it was with most of the moving spirits of the '90s, but with none more than Henry Harland. The polishing of his prose was for him his being's end and aim, and I have often seen him at that sacred task of a forenoon, in his study-bedroom, still in pyjamas and dressing-gown, with a coffee-pot on the hearth, bending over an exquisite piece of handwriting, like a goldsmith at his bench. It was his theory that the brain was freshest immediately after rising, and he was jealous of dissipating that morning energy by any activities of the toilet, leaving his bath and his breakfast, which with him, of course, was *déjeuner*, till the real business of the day, a page of "perfect prose," was accomplished. Not always a page, by any means—a perfect sentence or two was sometimes a good morning's work; which recalls Wilde's jest about a hard day's work: "This morning," he said, "I took out a comma, and this afternoon—I put it in again."

Such meticulous craftsmanship is unfashionable nowadays. As Stevenson once prophetically wrote to me: "The little, artificial popularity of style in England tends, I think, to die out; the British pig returns to his true love, the love of the styleless, of the shapeless, of the slapdash and the disorderly." We are very much at ease in Zion, and affect the slapdash and the disorderly, if we have it not. We are of Dogberry's opinion that to write comes by nature, and, of course, it is true that no amount of sedulous aping can make a writer if he is not born to write; but that is one thing, and to leave all to nature is another. Of course, some writers even of "finished art" are more spontaneous than others, and too much self-consciousness about style may defeat its own aim, and become a nervous obsession. After all, the product, not the process, is what concerns the reader, and, so long as the process does not "stick out," it is only the writer's affair how arduous or how casual it is. But that the writers of the '90s should have taken their "art" seriously and have striven to make it as fine as possible cannot reasonably be urged against them. Anyhow, in Harland's case, to the extent of his achievement, the end justified the means, and, though his work may not be as important as he hoped it was, yet it still retains its charming place, and would certainly have been no better if he had aimed—a curious aim, surely, for any writer—at the styleless and shapeless, the slapdash and the disorderly. That spontaneity was his, too, his delightful familiar letters bear witness. One of these, a prose lyric in praise of Paris—*à propos* a visit to that city which I once paid him and his charming wife—I transcribe here:

GRAND CAFÉ RESTAURANT DE LA PAIX
5 PLACE DE L'OPERA
PARIS, *wednesday*.

Do, my Dear Le Gallienne, do come and join us in this enchanted town, where the sun shines, and the coffee-houses prosper, and everybody has the Artistic Temperament, more or less. It would be such fun for us, and it couldn't but do you good. And you would be sure to live, as well as write, all manner of delectable things in prose and verse. The only pretty English word I can remember for the moment is Come; so I repeat it—Come, come, come. Aline and I are seated at this moment on the terrace of the Café de la Paix— and I am writing on my knee, which accounts for the tremulousness of my hand. And we are both wishing hard that you were here—where, if there is anything in telepathy, you will be moved to flit across the Manche. We are drinking iced coffee, because the air is hot; and such a funny motley crowd is surging backwards and forwards on the pavement—Infidels, Jews, and Turks, as well as Christian English and Parisians—priests, soldiers, bourgeois, and prostitutes. It is most diverting; and, once here, you will wonder how you have lived elsewhere. Therefore—Come. We will spend laborious days and tavern nights. We will dine with Dauphin Meunier, and sup with dear old Verlaine, and breakfast with the Muses. We'll walk in the Bois de Boulogne, loaf in the Boulevards, listen to the Band in the Luxembourg, and enjoy ourselves *partout*. So, at the risk of seeming a votary of damnable iteration I must again say Come. Our address is 35, Rue de Lubeck. Send us a line when to expect you.

Always yours, H. HARLAND.

During my stay with Harland in Paris we were joined by Hubert Crackanthorpe, another amateur of the short story, whose "Wreckage" was one of the sensations of the period. Crackanthorpe's concern was not with his prose, but with the faithful presentation of human character and story, as close to the bare fact as possible, with no intrusion whatever of the writer's temperament. A scrupulous, almost fanatical, "objectivity" was his artistic aim. It was the ideal of Guy de Maupassant, who was very much "the master" just then, and Crackanthorpe followed it with such severity as, it seems to me, to give his work a certain hardness and dryness, and even lack of atmosphere. One felt that his characters and situations were presented too much as in a vacuum. Some suffusion of his austerely suppressed self might have endued it with more magnetism. That self was, indeed, strangely different from his work, so gentle, and chivalric, and romantic. His lovable boyish presence must still haunt many memories, as his tragic death, mysteriously self-sought in the Seine—for he seemed the happiest of fortunate youth—is still an open wound for those to whom he was unforgettably dear.

Perhaps the most valuable success of *The Yellow Book* lay in the excellence and variety of its short stories, and in its introduction to a wider public of so many admirable artists in that form. Among these the most notable was Mrs. George Egerton, whose "Keynotes" was one of the memorable sensations of the time, Marriott Watson, Maurice Baring, Kenneth Grahame, Charles Kennett Burrow, Evelyn Sharp, Netta Syrett, and Ella D'Arcy.

Curiously enough the one name we, of all others, should have expected to find there, the "yellowest" of all, is missing—that of Oscar Wilde. Of him, as the dominating figure of the period, it is time to speak.

My acquaintance with Oscar Wilde began in my pre-London days as a member of an audience in Birkenhead, the sister city to Liverpool, assembled to hear him lecture on his "Impressions of America," whence he had recently returned. He had not then published anything except his first volume of poems, and was known only as the "apostle" of aestheticism, the prototype of Bunthorne in "Patience," a ridiculous, posturing figure, a fanastic laughing-stock, whom no one took seriously. And yet I am glad to record to the credit of that Birkenhead audience, that, after its first bewilderment, it forgot to laugh at him, and soon began laughing with him, and I remember how grateful I was to my father, the last man I expected to be impressed, for saying, as the lecture ended: "Don't make any mistake. That man is no fool."

At that time Wilde had abandoned his knee-breeches and was dressed in a sort of Georgian costume, with tight pantaloon trousers and a huge stock. His amber-coloured hair, naturally straight, was not very long, and was unashamedly curled and massively modelled to his head, somewhat suggesting a wig. His large figure, with his big loose face, grossly jawed with thick, sensuous lips, and a certain fat effeminacy about him, suggested a sort of caricature Dionysius disguised as a rather heavy dandy of the Regency period. There was something grotesquely excessive about his whole appearance, and while he was in a way handsome, he made one think of an enormous doll, a preposterous, exaggerated puppet such as smile foolishly from floats at the Nice carnival. But his strong, humorous haughty eyes, his good brow and fine nose must not be forgotten from the general effect, nor his superb and rather insolent *aplomb*, which early dominated his audience. And, of course, his wonderful golden voice, which he modulated with elaborate self-consciousness. Exotic as he was, he was at the same time something entirely different from the dilettante, lily-like "aesthete" we had expected, and the great surprise about him was his impudent humour and sound common sense. That he could talk sense at all was a complete revelation. Bunthorne, indeed, had not remotely suggested anything like this boyish fun, or such searching yet laughable social criticism, and such reasonable ideas on all possible subjects. There was, too, an unquestionable fascination about the strange popinjay who said things all we youngsters had been dimly feeling, and who

even won our parents into the involuntary admission
that he was "no fool." It was only natural that when
one of these youngsters published a volume of poems
of his own, he should send a copy to this friend of
dreaming and rebellious youth, suddenly dropped out
of the sky into that very British and humdrum Birkenhead; and that the flattering letter of acknowledgment
which presently followed, in that exquisite handwriting of Wilde's which made English look beautiful as
Greek, and the like of which had certainly never come
through the Birkenhead mail before, should have had
no little of the quality of a fairy tale. In that letter
Wilde had asked me to come and take tea with him
and Mrs. Wilde, when next I was in London, and it
was not long after my arrival there that I found myself
one spring afternoon on my way to "16, Tite Street,
Chelsea," a street that Whistler had already made
famous.

I remember that my first feeling at seeing Wilde
again was one of boyish disappointment. He didn't
seem as "romantic" as when I had seen him at Birkenhead. His Regency clothes had gone, and he wore a
prosaic business suit of some commonplace cloth,
tweeds I almost fear. His hair, too, was short and
straight, no Dionysiac curls. Also I had a queer feeling
of distaste, as my hand seemed literally to sink into his,
which were soft and plushy. I never recall those lines
in "The Sphinx"—

Lift up your large black satin eyes,
Which are like cushions where one sinks,

without thinking of Wilde's hands. However, this

feeling passed off as soon as he began to talk. One secret of the charm of Wilde's talk, apart from its wit and his beautiful voice, was the evidently sincere interest he took in his listener and what he also had to say. It is seldom that a good talker can listen too, and for this reason even great talkers often end in being bores. Wilde was a better artist in this respect, though I am convinced that it was not merely art. With all his egoism, he had an unselfish sympathetic side to him which was well known to his friends, in whose affairs, particularly their artistic projects, he seemed entirely to forget his own. Even in his more elaborate flights of decorated talk, he was never a monopolist. He was always ready to stop and hear someone else. He had none of that impatient patience of some talkers, who seem only waiting till one's remarks are over to resume their own eloquence, as though we had never spoken. Such conversational amenity is a rare grace. With Wilde it came easily, for one reason, because of his intellectual curiosity. His interest in others was not a gossipy interest. What concerned him chiefly was their characters and minds, particularly what they were thinking, or, if they were artists, what they were doing. Naturally, this made him a very agreeable companion, and for a boy from "the provinces" to have this sophisticated man of letters listening so respectfully to his plans for poems and so forth, on which, he immediately began to draw me out, was no little flattering. One of the first things he asked me about was my age. Twenty-three, I told him.

"Twenty-three!" he commented, with a dramatic sigh. "It is a kind of genius to be twenty-three!"

Who that has long since passed that inspired age will

deny that this was as much a truth as a phrase—which, indeed, was usually the case with even Wilde's most frivolous phrases.

After we had talked for a while in his study, we went upstairs to the drawing-room where Mrs. Wilde sat with their two boys. Mrs. Wilde was a pretty young woman of the innocent Kate Greenaway type. They seemed very happy together, though it was impossible not to predict suffering for a woman so simple and domestic mated with a mind so searching and so perverse and a character so self-indulgent. It was hard to see where two such different natures could find a meeting-place, particularly as poor Mrs. Wilde was entirely devoid of humour and evangelically religious. So sweet and pretty and good, how came she by her outrageously intellectual husband, to whose destructive wit little was sacred and all things comedy? When one thinks that Mrs. Wilde's chief interest after her children was—missionaries, and her bosom friend that Lady Sandhurst, who was one of the pillars of British church work . . . !

"Missionaries, my dear!" I remember Wilde once saying at a dinner party. "Don't you realize that missionaries are the divinely provided food for destitute and underfed cannibals? Whenever they are on the brink of starvation, Heaven, in its infinite mercy, sends them a nice plump missionary." To which Mrs. Wilde could only pathetically exclaim: "Oh, Oscar! you cannot surely be in earnest. You can only be joking."

No one present remarked that the Reverend Sydney Smith had indulged in a like humour when he spoke of "a slice of cold missionary on the sideboard." Wilde, like all wits, was occasionally indebted to his forerunners, though the implication of Whistler's famous "You will say it, Oscar" is, of course, absurd. Wilde was under no necessity of borrowing from Whistler or anyone else, though, like everyone, he would now and again elaborate on ideas which he had rather made his own than originated. For example, that same evening, he was talking of criticism, and saying that a critic of literature should not feel bound down by his subject, but should merely use whatever author he was discussing, or reviewing, as a starting-point for the expression of his own individuality. On which I innocently asked him if he had read M. Anatole France's "La Vie Littéraire"! He looked at me with rather haughty surprise:

"You have read Anatole France!" he said.

Who would have expected a provincial young man from Liverpool to be so unseasonably acquainted with a certain *mot* about the adventures of a critic's soul among masterpieces which had then been made only a very short time. It was mean of me, I admit.

But to return to Mrs. Wilde and the children in the drawing-room. Wilde was then in the period of his first fairy tales, and those beautifully simple and innocent stories in "The Happy Prince" volume were shortly to be published.

"It is the duty of every father," he said with great gravity, "to write fairy tales for his children. But the mind of a child is a great mystery. It is incalculable, and who shall divine it, or bring to it its own peculiar delights? You humbly spread before it the treasures of your imagination, and they are as dross. For example, a day or two ago, Cyril yonder came to me with the question, 'Father, do you ever dream?' 'Why of course,

my darling. It is the first duty of a gentleman to dream.'
'And what do you dream of?' asked Cyril, with a child's
disgusting appetite for facts. Then I, believing, of
course, that something picturesque would be expected
of me, spoke of magnificent things: 'What do I dream
of? Oh, I dream of dragons with gold and silver scales,
and scarlet flames coming out of their mouths, of
eagles with eyes made of diamonds that can see over
the whole world at once, of lions with yellow manes,
and voices like thunder, of elephants with little houses
on their backs, and tigers and zebras with barred and
spotted coats. . . .' So I laboured on with my fancy, till,
observing that Cyril was entirely unimpressed, and
indeed quite undisguisedly bored, I came to a humiliat-
ing stop, and, turning to my son there, I said: 'But tell
me, what do you dream of, Cyril?' His answer was like
a divine revelation: 'I dream of *pigs*,' he said."

Wilde had a charming gift of improvising, or seeming to improvise, fables to illustrate points of view
often no less improvised for the occasion. Some of
these he afterwards printed, but many others must
have lived and died as he created them, out of his
fertile picture-making thought. One I recall from that
first afternoon that I have not seen or heard of since.
He was talking of free will, which he regarded as an
illusion. Destiny, from which none could excape, ruled
us all, he was saying. And then he went on:

"Once upon a time there was a magnet, and in its
close neighbourhood lived some steel filings. One day
two or three little filings felt a sudden desire to go and
visit the magnet, and they began to talk of what a
pleasant thing it would be to do. Other filings near by
overheard their conversation, and they, too, became

infected with the same desire. Still others joined them, till at last all the filings began to discuss the matter, and more and more their vague desire grew into an impulse.

" 'Why not go to-day?' said some of them: but others were of opinion that it would be better to wait till to-morrow. Meanwhile, without their having noticed it, they had been involuntarily moving nearer to the magnet, which lay there quite still, apparently taking no heed of them. And so they went on discussing, all the time insensibly drawing nearer to their neighbour; and the more they talked, the more they felt the impulse growing stronger, till the more impatient ones declared that they would go that day, whatever the rest did. Some were heard to say that it was their duty to visit the magnet, and that they ought to have gone long ago. And, while they talked, they moved always nearer and nearer, without realizing that they had moved. Then, at last, the impatient ones prevailed, and, with one irresistible impulse, the whole body cried out, 'There is no use waiting. We will go to-day. We will go now. We will go at once.' And then in one unanimous mass they swept along, and in another moment were clinging fast to the magnet on every side. Then the magnet smiled—for the steel filings had no doubt at all but that they were paying that visit of their own free will."

I grew to know Wilde very well, and have many memories of his charming companionship and of the generous friendship he gave me in those early days before the clouds began to settle about his life. Though there were those whom he repelled, most of his acquaintance came under the spell of his extra-

Letter from Oscar Wilde to Mrs. Ada Leverson
[Bosie is Lord Alfred Douglas]

ordinary personality. For all his sophistication, there was in him a great simplicity. Strange as it may sound, he was an unusually natural creature, and what were regarded as affectations and eccentricities came of his being himself as few have the courage to be—"an art which nature makes." His poses were self-dramatizations, of which he expected others to see the fun, as he invariably saw it himself. Moreover, there was reality behind them all, and it was only because his way of looking at things was so new to his day that they seemed fantastic. He employed exaggeration merely as a means of conveying his intellectual sincerity, and, as I once said, paradox with him was merely Truth standing on its head to attract attention. Behind all his humorous fopperies there was a serious philosophy, as beneath all the surface sophistication there was the deep and simple heart of a poet. Doubtless, he was weak as well as strong, and wrong as he was right, but, if there was evil in him, there was also a great good. His success developed a dangerous arrogance, and he lost the captainship of his soul, but that his soul was essentially pure and his heart tender, no one who knew him well could for a moment doubt. I knew him well and am proud to have been his friend.

When his downfall came, a tragedy which, when one considers its nature and extent, he bore with remarkable fortitude, I was already in America, and my memories of him are confined to the sunlit days of his early successes. When I think of him it is as a victorious, happy figure, always gay, always with some witty nonsense on his tongue. His gaiety was not so much in his manner, in which it amused him to affect an almost ostentatious gravity, a humorous gravity, however, which none could mistake. It was the unfailing gaiety of his mind that was so captivating. One never left him without carrying away some characteristic *mot*, light as thistledown, yet usually pregnant with meaning.

I think it was Meredith who said that "some flowers have roots deep as oaks," and the phrase might be fitly applied to most of Wilde's talk; as, for instance, when he said, in reference to literature as a possible intercessor between rival nations, that he hoped some day, when men had become sufficiently civilized, it would seem natural to say, "We will not go to war with France—because her prose is perfect," a phrase which needs little pondering for one to see how deep it goes. But the *mots* of his which I recall at random were mainly happy nonsense, though usually uttered with imperturbable seriousness.

One day, as he stood outside his Tite Street door, preparing to insert his latchkey, a little humble man came up, saying that he had called about the taxes.

"Taxes!" said Wilde, looking down at him from his lordly height. "Why should I pay taxes?"

"But, sir,". said the little man, "you are the householder here, are you not? . . . You live here—you sleep here?"

"Ah, yes!" said Wilde, with utter solemnity, "but then, you see—I sleep so badly!"

On another occasion, as he walked in the Haymarket, a beggar came up and asked for alms. He had, he said, no work to do and no bread to eat.

"Work!" said Wilde. "Why should you want to work? And bread! Why should you eat bread?"

Then, after an elaborate pause, he continued, putting his hand good-naturedly on the tatterdemalion's shoulder:

"Now, if you had come to me and said that you had work to do, but you couldn't dream of working, and that you had bread to eat, but couldn't think of eating bread—I would have given you half-a-crown."—Another pause—"As it is, I give you two shillings."

So Wilde, with his accustomed generosity, made the poor fellow happy and had his own little joke in the bargain.

The reference to the Haymarket reminds me of Tree's theatre, and the first night of his Hamlet, which, like all Hamlet first nights, was a very serious occasion. Of course, Wilde was there, and went behind to see Tree, who, all excitement, perspiration, and grease paint, eagerly asked, "Well, Oscar, what do you think of my Hamlet?" Wilde assumed his gravest, most pontifical air, and, spacing out his words with long pauses of even more than his usual deliberation, as though he was almost too impressed to speak at all, he said:

"My dear Tree—I think—your—Hamlet . . . your —Hamlet, my dear Tree . . . I think—your—Hamlet" —Tree, meanwhile, hanging expectant on each slow-dropping word, nervous and keyed up as most actors are on a first night, anxiously filling the pauses with "Yes, yes, my dear Oscar . . ." while Wilde continued to keep him on tenterhooks with further preliminary ejaculations of "My dear Tree," and "I think your Hamlet." At last, when he could hold the suspended compliment no longer, Wilde ended with: "My dear Tree—I—think—your Hamlet . . . is . . . *funny* . . . *without—being vulgar!*"

In many of his *mots* Wilde had a remarkable skill in making bricks without straw, or catching up any wind-blown straw for his purpose with fascinating readiness. It was that skill which gave his wit so incomparable a levity. His "Intentions" were published in London by Osgood, McIlvaine & Co., a new firm that made a point in all their advertisements of the fact that all their books were "published simultaneously in London and New York." That was their "slogan," as the advertising men put it. Well, one morning I happened to meet Wilde in Piccadilly. After our first greetings, he assumed an air of deep grief: "Did you see in the papers, this morning," he said, "that Osgood is dead?" He paused for a moment, his manner deepening in solemnity, and continued: "Poor Osgood! He is a great loss to us! However," he added, as with consolatory cheerfulness, "I suppose they will bury him simultaneously in London and New York!"

Another delightfully foolish remark I recall *à propos* Mr. Kipling's "Captains Courageous," which, it will be remembered, is concerned with a lad's adventures among the cod fishers off the Banks of Newfoundland.

"I really don't know," said Wilde, "why an author should write a book all about cod-fishing." Then, after a pause, in which he seemed to be thinking it over, he said, as by way of explanation: "But perhaps it is because—I never eat cod!"—the possibility of eating cod being too vulgar to contemplate.

The story of his appearance before the curtain on the first night of "Lady Windermere's Fan" is well known—how he stood in front of the stage, in light evening overcoat, his opera hat in one hand, and the smoke from a lighted cigarette mounting from the other, and gravely congratulated the audience on the great success it had made that evening in so intelligently appreciating his play.

He had sent me two stalls for the occasion, with a characteristic note of invitation to my wife and myself, which ran: "DEAR POET—here are two stalls for my play. Come, and bring your poem to sit beside you."

Between the acts I went up to the theatre bar for a drink, and there was Wilde in the midst of a group of his admiring disciples, over whom he towered head and shoulders. On catching sight of me he left them and came over to me.

"My dear Richard," he said, "where have you been? It seems as if we hadn't met for years. Now tell me what you have been doing."

But, before I could answer, he assumed an air of concern. "Oh, yes!" he said. "I remember. I have a crow to pick with you."

Though I suspected some jest, I, too, affected concern.

"Yes," he continued, "you recently published a book called 'The Religion of a Literary Man.' "

I nodded.

"Well," he went on, "you were very unkind to me in that book," and he put on an air of deep grievance, "most unkind!"

"My dear Oscar—" I began.

"Oh, yes, you were, and you know it," he reiterated.

"I unkind to you!" I said, beginning to be really mystified.

"Most unkind. I could not believe it of you—so unkind to so true a friend."

So he continued to lure me on into the trap he had suddenly improvised for me. I stood pondering what it was I could have done, for I began to think he was serious.

"Why, Oscar," I said at last, "I don't know what you mean. Unkind to you in 'The Religion of a Literary Man' . . . why, I can't remember that I even mentioned your name in it."

Then he laughed out, with huge enjoyment of the success of his little stratagem:

"Ah! Richard, that was just it."

Then, having drunk together, this serious explanation over, he resumed:

"But do tell me, what else have you been writing?" I told him that, among other things, I had been writing an essay on loving my enemies.

"That's a great theme. I should like to write on that, too. For, do you know, all my life I have been looking for twelve men who didn't believe in me . . . and, so far, I have only found eleven."

It was not till long after that I reflected on the strangely prophetic significance of that lightly uttered speech, the merest badinage of the moment; for, when a friend brought me the news of Wilde's sentence, I said: "Poor Oscar! he has found his twelfth man."

Looking back on that tragedy, I sometimes wonder whether it did not mean more to Wilde's friends than it meant to himself. Indeed, inordinately fond of the limelight as he was, so conscious throughout his career of his own drama, one cannot help the suspicion that he rather enjoyed his own tragedy. And in a sense, aside from its social inconvenience, and he being what he was, it is possible to understand his doing so. For he had been condemned at the bar of a Philistine public opinion whose jurisdiction he regally denied. Despising the public, while at the same time its attention was the breath of his nostrils, it was hardly to be expected that he should take its condemnation seriously. It was, doubtless, disagreeable, for the storm he had raised must have seemed more furious and trying to his courage than he had foreseen, but not important. The ostracism from that society at whose pleasant dinner tables he had been the king must have been to him its greatest hardship—the real "hard labour" of his sentence. Perhaps he sometimes recalled his own phrase that to be in society was a bore but to be outside it a tragedy. It is one's suspicion of this attitude which robs "De Profundis" of its convincingness, hard as Wilde worked to convey the impression of a broken and a contrite heart. Wilde's heart was probably neither, but his vanity was at once impaled and flattered. How could he regard himself as a criminal when his intellect did not accept the standards by which he had been judged and condemned? No "conversion" could have taken place in a brain like his. To him his offence would merely represent a difference of taste in morals, with no essential wrong in it. The penalty for this difference was indeed hard, but it was a necessary part of his drama. It left him spiritually and intellectually unchanged, and he probably considered himself a martyr to Philistine stupidity and ignorance of physiology rather than a criminal. He had haughtily defied the lightning, and even when it struck him, he must have examined its bolts with intellectual curiosity and contempt. Indeed, it is not unlikely that he had counted on their inability effectually to strike him, for success, which had become a disease with him, had made him so insanely arrogant that he probably felt himself capable, so to say, of bluffing the British Empire; and when we consider the posthumous triumphs of his personality, it looks very much as if he had not entirely miscalculated.

Wilde once said that he gave only his talent to his writings, and kept his genius for his conversation. This was quite true, but it would have been truer still if he had said that he kept his genius for his life; for his writings, the value of which is less than he thought, and more than some allow, are but one illustrative part of him. They contribute to the general effect he strove to produce, the dramatization of his own personality. From the beginning to the end he was a great actor—of himself.

As that self, for good or ill, summoned up so completely the various aspects and tendencies of his time, he has become its symbolic figure. He is, beyond comparison, the incarnation of the spirit of the '90s. The significance of the '90s is that they began to apply all the new ideas that had been for some time accumulating from the disintegrating action of scientific and philosophic thought on every kind of spiritual, moral, social and artistic convention, and all forms of authority demanding obedience merely as authority. Hence came that widespread assertion and demonstration of individualism which is still actively progressing. Wilde was the synthesis of all these phenomena of change. He may be said to have included Huxley and Pater and Morris and Whistler and Mr. Bernard Shaw and Mr. Max Beerbohm in the amazing eclecticism of his extravagant personality, that seems to have borrowed everything and made everything his own. Out of the 1890 chaos he emerged an astonishing, impudent microcosm.

In him the period might see its own face in a glass. And it is because it did see its own face in him that it first admired, then grew afraid, and then destroyed him. Here, said the moralist, is where your "modern" ideas will lead you, and the moralist, as often, was both right and wrong. Wilde did gaily and flippantly what some men were doing in dead earnest, with humour and wit for his weapons. What serious reformers had laboured for years to accomplish Wilde did in a moment with the flash of an epigram. He was like that *enfant terrible* in Andersen's fairy tale who called out, "Why, the king has nothing on," and while his audience laughed, it awakened, and the truth beneath his phrases went home. Indeed, he made dying Victorianism laugh at itself, and it may be said to have died of the laughter.

I have called the '90s "romantic," not merely because it was romantic to have lived in them, or because they included so many romantic figures, but because their representative writers and artists emphasized the modern determination to escape from the deadening thraldom of materialism and outworn conventions, and to live life significantly—keenly and beautifully, personally and, if need be, daringly; to win from it its fullest satisfactions, its deepest and richest and most exhilarating experiences. The will to romance: that, in a phrase, was the motive philosophy of the '90s.

INDEX

Page

INDEX

INDEX

INDEX